# Growing

**Abby Thompson**

Growing

Olympia Publishers
*London*

www.olympiapublishers.com
OLYMPIA PAPERBACK EDITION

Copyright © Abby Thompson 2024

The right of Abby Thompson to be identified as the author of
this work has been asserted in accordance with sections 77 and 78 of
the Copyright, Designs and Patents Act 1988.

**All Rights Reserved**

No reproduction, copying, or transmission of this publication
may be made without written permission.
No paragraph of this publication may be reproduced,
copied or transmitted save with the written permission of the publisher,
or in accordance with the provisions
of the Copyright Act 1956 (as amended).

Any person who commits any unauthorized act in relation to
this publication may be liable to criminal
prosecution and civil claims for damage.

A CIP catalogue record for this title is
available from the British Library.

ISBN: 978-1-80439-967-5

This is a work of fiction.
Names, characters, places and incidents originate from the writer's imagination. Any resemblance to actual persons, living or dead, is purely coincidental.

First Published in 2024

Olympia Publishers
Tallis House
2 Tallis Street
London
EC4Y 0AB

Printed in Great Britain

# Dedication

I dedicate this book to the authors who made me fall in love with reading years ago. Your words have inspired me to find my own.

# Preface

Any dedicated fan of the iconic TV show *Friends* is sure to recite memorable lines from the series frequently; it's practically a rite of passage. My initiation into the world of *Friends* happened back in high school with my family, as we watched the entire series on DVD. Since then, a day hasn't gone by without at least catching a snippet of the show.

Strangely enough, it took nearly a decade for me to focus on the title sequence, also known as the theme song. Only then did I begin to understand its surprisingly profound lyrics, which resonate deeply with the trials of young adulthood. The opening verse, "So no one told you life was gonna be this way," succinctly captures the essence of existence: the unexpected challenges, the perpetual state of growth, and the shared journey of navigating life with others to the best of our abilities.

Up until this moment, I had a fixed belief that growth was a linear journey with a definite endpoint: adulthood. I naively anticipated a clear distinction between childhood and maturity, yet reality quickly, and somewhat harshly, proved otherwise. Accepting the immense variability in life paths has been a challenging truth to embrace. The process of growing has proven to be a far more complex and uncertain experience than I had ever envisioned. The much-anticipated milestone between youth and adulthood turned out to be an elusive and shifting concept rather than a tangible moment that I once thought it would be. Now, the road ahead stretches endlessly like an unending run-on sentence with no punctuation in sight. The future I once fantasized about is now my reality, but the actuality is vastly different from what I envisioned.

During my senior year of college, I began to wonder if anyone actually feels like they've made it, or is it completely relative? What is making it, and who decides if you have or haven't? Is life just one big guessing game? I innocently thought when I graduated from college, I would finally feel my age, things would click, and I would obtain some aspect of self-actualization. That by this point my head and heart would be synced.

When I was a little girl I thought frequently about my early twenties and what it would be like, dreaming of the confident assurance I would somehow obtain. I thought by now I would've had it figured out, but boy, was I wrong. This stage of life feels like learning how to walk again. Of course I don't remember learning to walk, but I can only imagine it was a frustrating experience. The steps taken are very wobbly at the beginning. I assume I ran ahead of myself, went too fast, and consequently fell many times. Maybe some days I was too scared to try. Learning how to get up again and keep going is the essence of adulthood—really of being human. Or as one of my all time favorite singers Frank Sinatra says, "Each time I find myself flat on my face, I pick myself up and get back in the race. That's life."

The challenge I am presently dealing with is figuring out how and where I want to walk. That is no small feat. Now my parents and other mentors can't and shouldn't make decisions for me. It's ironic because, as all children do, I hated when my parents told me what to do and now I wish they would. Coming of age feels unnatural at times because it's when you begin to find out who you really are without any forced influence. What you believe, think, and do is up to you now. No one can come save the day anymore. As exciting as that is, it's undeniably scary as well. None of us set out to mess up but it's inevitable. No one wants to be wrong, but a lot of the time we are. As a perfectionist, I don't like thinking about the fact that I will drop the ball at some point, many times. With constant existential questions floating around and looping in my head, I knew I needed to channel them in some way. I began to journal, which turned into what you are reading. To say I'm putting everything out there is an understatement. Before deciding to turn my very private thoughts into a public book, I kept coming back to this question: Do my words matter? I assume most authors ask themselves this. Frankly, why would anyone want to read essays about a young American Gen Z's privileged white girl's experience into adulthood? I came up with a couple of reasons.

One, the sentiment and advice any artist or creator hears countless times is create what you need. As an avid reader myself, I wanted a book like this when I first began to ask myself these questions but could not find it. I found books on practical advice into adulthood written by people double my age, which is great and necessary, but I never found something as personal as what I wanted. I never set out to write this book or any book for that matter. I have no experience and honestly I don't know if I ever made an A on a paper in school. I wrote to process all of the paradoxical emotions I'm trying to make sense of, and it has been cathartic in ways that I can't adequately put words to. It gave me purpose and structure to my life that felt like it had none at the time. People talk about their struggles often times in past tense. I didn't want that. I didn't want to read a book about someone who has "figured it out" or who "knows how to maximize their life" in just the right way. I wanted someone to say, I see you, and I get it.

    Secondly, I believe that every person on the planet has a specific and unique purpose for their life. If you're breathing you still have work to do here. The most pressing question most young adults' face is what am I going to do to make this world a better place? Where do I fit in, and how am I going to make a difference? My words matter because I would not be here if they didn't. What I do matters. The things I am passionate about matter. No matter how big or small your circle is you have influence despite any obstacle you might face, and obstacles usually turn into your greatest asset when stewarded well. They qualify you to be where you are because no one likes perfect people. Well no one likes to be around people that think they're perfect. If anyone has made you feel less than worthy and valuable, shame on them. You, and what you care about, are here for a reason.

    So that is why I fought back against the absolute absurdity in writing a book when I had no idea on how to do it. To show people that your words matter just as much as anyone else's. That you can do hard things even when you think you can't. We all already have a seat at the table, but it is up to us to find the courage to pull out a chair, sit, and take up space in whatever area you're dreaming for. I have courageously pulled out my writer's chair to share my heart with whoever reads this. I can only hope that you will pull out yours, stay a while, and listen.

# Introduction

The most powerful word to me is "why." Yet, also one of the hardest to explain because often times the answer is unclear and dependent on who you ask. Which I hate. As a child there were always answers to my questions, and I wrongly assumed that's how the rest of my life would go. When that far away day came and I magically turned into an adult, (which I secretly never could picture), I would have figured out a lot of the "why's" just like my parents and other parental figures seemingly did. I thought that by having a high school and college degree, and constantly trying to educate myself by reading, listening, and watching things I deem important, I would know some things. People even tell me how seemingly wise and mature I am for my age, but it's odd because the more I learn, the less I feel like I know.

Over time I've learned that knowledge is power, and I want to soak in as much of it as I can. As you will see later in this book, my questions, imagination, and curiosity were not channeled in a positive way for a long time. I was so obsessed with what could go wrong that I couldn't fully enjoy the things that were going right. I finally realized, with a lot of help from family and therapists, if I can worry I can wonder. Although I am nowhere near perfect, every day, I try to use my imagination for good and the words you're reading are evidence of that.

One of my favorite questions to ask people—young, old, man or woman—is: 'Do you feel your age?' Shockingly, or maybe not, most people say they don't. Almost everyone feels much younger than they are. The follow-up question usually is, at what point are you grown, or when did you feel grown up? Some say when they had their own kids. Some when they got their first "real" job. I began to wonder is it really that concrete? As a child, I would think about all of the milestones ahead of me and how I couldn't wait to get there. I was sure that once I got to these physical markers like driving, going to college, or getting a job, I would feel like I had made it. Like I wasn't still a kid pretending to be an adult. I was very surprised to find out that once I achieved these things, graduating into adulthood per say, I didn't feel any different. I'm still me.

I vividly remember my parents telling me on more than one occasion to not wish my life away. I would roll my eyes and go back to whatever I was doing, not understanding what they meant. Years later, I not only understand, I also now embrace that to the best of my ability. One day at a time. Thinking much further beyond that is too overwhelming and to a degree unnecessary. However with the cultural climate we live in, staying present is increasingly difficult as each day goes by. We bounce from one thing to the next without appreciating, or maybe even realizing, what just happened. As I enter into young adulthood, a life goal of mine is to be as present in any given moment as I possibly can be because once a moment is gone, it's gone forever.

I've never given much thought to why I love photography so much, and why I am constantly snapping photos and videos of my life and the lives of people around me. I think it's because it's the only way to semi-relive a moment for what it truly was; which led me to the acute realization that life only has one gear shift. No reverse. No break. Just drive. There is no re-living a moment. As I began to realize this, I wanted to ask anyone and everyone on how they go after living a purposeful life. I quickly learned a good life isn't something we can be taught, which is very unnerving to me. I want to get life right. I want to know that I am doing the best I can, that I'm making the most of my every day, and that I'm on the right path, but the only person that can decide that is me.

I began to worry if I was doing something wrong, not processing my emotions correctly because when big life events happen, one of the only feelings that comes over me is disbelief. I was the kid who so desperately wanted to be an adult, so why does it feel so weird being one? Being thirteen years old in the eighth-grade daydreaming about being twenty-three living in New York City felt unfathomable. In my underdeveloped child brain, I somehow thought that I would be a kid forever and my parents and other older adults would subsequently never age either. I felt like I was in some sort of time warp that only included me. Am I crazy for thinking this?

As far back as my memory goes, I have always wanted to grow up. Believe me, or ask anyone I grew up with, I have acted and thought I was an adult since I was a baby and have always thoroughly enjoyed that role. I have played mother toward my sister since I was two. (She apparently only took a bottle when I gave it to her, and I am still proud of that.) I am a very independent introvert and have never enjoyed typical teenage and young adult things, such as pretending like consequences don't apply to you, so why is actually becoming what I've seemingly always wanted to be harder than I expected?

When I went to college and felt all of the emotions about the life changes to come, like moving away for the first time, I tried to dive deep into what I thought I was supposed to feel, but it just wasn't that deep to me. The scene in the movie *The Holiday* with

Cameron Diaz, when she tries to make herself cry but gives up, is the epitome of me and how I felt at that time. I was the most prepared for that transition, high school to college, and was not thrown off guard at all. Four years later, though, I am beginning to feel the effects of what it means to be completely moving on from childhood and the security of the school system, the only structure I've ever known.

The idea of growing is so much more abstract than I ever thought it could be. Sure, we all have our own complexes about growing up and fears about what the future looks like, but ultimately for me it boils down to the loss of innocence, the ability to become jaded, and the fact that time does not stop for anything or anyone. Regardless of how I feel about the passage of time, it passes. We are all on a clock, and although that probably sounds morbid to some, recognizing that allows even the mundane parts of life to become meaningful. I'm not looking for concrete answers to every single philosophical question, and definitely not trying to give them, but writing in real-time about what it feels like to be in the middle of child and adult. This pre-adult phase that isn't talked about enough.

We all view the world by the stories we've lived and told; that's why they're so powerful. We feel the most seen and understood when we realize the things that make us feel so alone are actually the things that unite us in an unexplainable way. I am not here to "should" anybody or convince you to think the way I do. My goal in writing this is for people to reflect on their own stories through my words, and maybe think about the things you've been denying yourself.

# Chapter One
## It's Just the Beginning

High school felt like a decade. Days felt like weeks and weeks, felt like months. I felt like growing up was never going to happen, or at the very least, it wasn't happening fast enough—until it was. Suddenly, life felt like it was moving in double time. College was a bit of a time warp because the pandemic happened right in the middle of it, and before I knew it my senior year was upon me. It's hard to believe these four years of college are rapidly coming to an end. Most endings feel that way. Our perception of time is distorted when things are wrapping up as opposed to being in the middle or beginning of something. It is that weird feeling of life flashing before your eyes quicker than you ever thought possible.

    As graduation approaches the door of childhood feels like it's quickly closing. And yes, I obviously know everyone in college is technically an adult but let's be honest. College students are not adults. We can pretend like we know what we're doing but we definitely don't. When something as big and impactful as childhood feels like it's dissipating, you can't help but feel sad. Where did the time go? When things change that are out of our control, we tend to want to grasp for the thing leaving much more than we would like to admit. When we think something or someone isn't going anywhere we don't miss it. This typically ends in us always wanting what we don't have. The finite nature of endings is scary, and I have a big one looming ahead.

## *Beginnings*

They are exciting; the middle can feel mundane, and the end comes quicker than we think it will. Most of us think we don't like the middle, the everyday, but we do. Normalcy and predictability are welcomed most of the time because it's comfortable, and we love to be comfortable. While the middle is important, beginnings and endings show us what we're made of. The middle is more predictable than what surrounds it, but the most growth tends to happen there.

The thought of childhood departing, the majority of my life thus far, terrifies me to a degree that doesn't feel normal. Children naturally have this protection around them where some things usually don't apply yet. Certain illnesses and responsibilities among other things are typically not in their demographic. As I will explain later in greater detail, I dealt with severe anxiety disorders off and on for a decent part of my childhood. Consequently, when someone with an abnormal amount of anxiety feels like any sort of protection is stripped away, it makes whatever is next feel scarier than it really is.

I realized the playfulness of childhood, which is arguably the best part, never has to fully go away, and it's something I want to take with me all throughout my life. Practically speaking, this looks like coloring and painting almost every day, just like I did as a kid. Am I good at it? No. But it's fun and reminds me that I don't have to be an expert at something to enjoy it. I have been a perfectionist since before I can remember. I did not talk at all until I was over two years old. I was so quiet for so long that my parents took me to get tested to make sure I didn't have a hearing disability. I did not, and soon after I turned two I started talking in full sentences. I never babbled or talked gibberish. I wanted to make sure I knew how to talk correctly before I did it. If you know me, you know how me this is. That's why I intentionally do things I am not good at, because I have had a hard time with it since the very beginning. We let kids have this freedom but adults not so much. Just because you have adult responsibilities doesn't mean you can't have a lighthearted and spontaneous personality. Allow yourself to not be so serious all of the time. I have to remind myself of this almost daily. I've been taking myself way too seriously since I can remember. Childish games? Not for me even as a six-year-old. Life is only as serious as you make it and it's important to take parts of every stage to the next one. For me that includes coloring and having stained hands most of the time.

Chapters of our stories should be revisited at one point or another, but to get to the next one we have to close the current. Chapters are never meant to stay open forever, but parts of them should be marked, highlighted, and taken along to help us navigate what's next. That is what I'm looking forward to—remembering and cherishing the past but not staying there.

If there was a book on how to achieve a perfect and pain-free life that was suitable for the entirety of the human race, there would be one by now. There are a lot of smart people in the world. That's the thing though, there isn't, and the people that think they've got it completely figured out are fools. That is one of the many exciting things about this stage; we now get our own opportunity to create and establish the best life we know how. This undeniably leaves ample room for failure, but with the help of the older and wiser it can make this confusing time a bit clearer. I'm confident older generations can remember back to the confusing transitional time that defines young adulthood.

## *The Gap*

There is a large generational gap if you have not noticed. I think about my grandparents and the dichotomy between how they grew up and the world they live in now and I honestly cannot imagine what that feels like. The way some have been able to adapt is very impressive, like my grandpa. He's seventy eight and one of my best friends on Snapchat. How much the world has changed in just fifty years is enough to make heads spin. I believe for the better. Of course I do, because I was born in 2000. Being born into the digital revolution with the amount of technology and access to a global community is incredible but impossible to grasp. Because of this, I understand how the baby boomers and Gen Z's don't always see eye to eye. I'm not sure we value the same things, but if we do, I don't think it is talked about very eloquently, or the way we go about it is different. It feels as if we can't understand each other. I wonder if it's that we won't not that we can't.

It comes down to a respect issue. You will never be able to understand someone if you do not first respect them. We live in a world where respect is similar to searching for a needle in a haystack. You will see metaphors a lot throughout this book. I'm from the American South, we love them. Dietrich Bonhoeffer, a German theologian during World War Two, put it this way. He says, "Nothing that we despise in the other man is entirely absent from ourselves. We must learn to regard people less in the light of what they do and more in the light of what they suffer from." Or, as Jordan Peterson puts it, "Set your house in perfect order before you criticize the world." Unless you're perfect, you have no room to judge anyone. It's overtly simple but clearly not easy. So much of life is like that.

The things you find rude, offensive, or whatever else, is most likely in you to some degree. We've all upset someone, probably multiple people, intentionally and unintentionally. It's odd that people think we have to agree on everything and if we don't, then the natural response is to give them no respect, much less befriend them. When did disagreeing with someone and hating them become synonymous? I'm genuinely asking. What is even more ironic is how we want all the grace and mercy possible for ourselves, but when it comes to others we demand justice. We learn the golden rule in preschool but tend to forget it. Treat others the way you want to be treated. If you want grace, you give it first. If you want respect, respect others.

If we want to influence people for the better it has to first start with respect, because as I have personally learned, no one will listen to you if they feel like you're judging them. People follow people not blanket statements, opinions, or facts. Once people feel heard only then will change be possible. Listening is the first, best, and most effective way to cultivate real and lasting change.

The early to mid-twenties is one of the few times in life where you can, in some ways, authentically connect with many generations. The teenage years weren't that long ago so the intense insecurity and annoyance of the world, I still understand. Walking through the hallway, hoping no one is staring at me, is a feeling I definitely haven't forgotten. I also have friends in their thirties that I couldn't be closer to, and coworkers in their fifties who I feel deeply connected to as they ask me for my thoughts on what their children, who are my age, might be thinking. Any sort of age difference feels substantial as a kid, but as the years go on they seem to even out. As a child it's hard to relate to anyone unless they are right around your age, but that isn't the case anymore. It's exciting to think about the endless amount of people that I can consider a friend, whether that be an eighteen-year-old or a sixty-year-old.

## *Conversations*

I love to have deep conversations with anyone that is willing to participate, especially if they have a different view than mine on something. There is so much value in listening and too many miss out on that. Friendly debates with family and friends are genuinely fun to me. I'm particularly good at starting something and then sitting back, listening, and watching everyone else get heated. I can imagine some of you have anxiety just thinking about that. I've noticed one particular phrase that the age range from fifty to seventy or older will say during some of these conversations, and it makes me smile. Before they start, they say, "These young kids," or "This generation is…" when they're talking about Gen-Z's. It's almost like we're aliens from some other planet that they've never seen before and cannot seem to grasp why we do the things we do, or why certain things are so important to us. This phrase doesn't offend me in the slightest because I get it. In a sense we are these strange people with new ideas, concepts, and world views.

My generation is the only one, thus far, that has been raised with all of the access of the internet and media we have today and are now growing into adults. I had Apple products and social media by the time I was ten years old. My dad, on the other hand, didn't even have a flip phone until after my sister was born, which was September 12th, 2001. Talk about a way to welcome a baby into the world. This event obviously rocked everyone and changed the way we see people today. When I hear people that can remember a life before that day talk about it, it's almost like there's a clear line in the sand: pre and post 9/11. What life was like then and what it is now.

I was born into a skeptical generation. Of course I can't personally speak to this, but it seems like back then people gave others the benefit of the doubt. That they assumed the best. We don't do that anymore. A defense mechanism my anxiety loves to use is seeing the worst in people first. (I swear I have friends—great ones, actually.) This really bothered me though so I brought it up to my therapist. Am I a terrible person? Why do I do this? She assures me I am not and says my brain is just trying to protect me from potential danger. We all do this to varying degrees, and how it manifests itself in our own lives looks different from person to person. I, for whatever reason, have always seen danger before I see safety. I see risk way before I see reward. The big events that shape one's generation, like 9/11 for me, impact the way I maneuver my way through the world. I view this place through a very incredulous lens.

Back to what I was saying, no other age group in the world thus far has grown up with the things my demographic did. I never navigated a "pre-cell phone and internet" world. Logically, it would make sense that we would act in a way that's different from what the older generations would classify as "normal." It doesn't bother me that my parents' friends, even my own parents and grandparents, say phrases like "Oh, these young kids just don't get it." What don't we get? How to work hard? No. There has been and always will be lazy people. This younger generation, though, has found very different and innovative ways to work, and that's undeniable. Remote working, having a huge salary just off of advertisements, a person being their own brand, and so on did not exist even twenty years ago. The "ideal" way to work now has never been done before, and that's what some older people don't seem get. It doesn't offend or upset me at all; it amuses me, if I am being honest, because it goes both ways. The rigidity in which many before us chose to live, not questioning or wondering about a different kind of life or system, seems odd to me, because that is what I've done my entire life: question. All of this to say, values and everyday life has changed drastically. Because of that, whether intentional or not, we have cut ourselves off from a very large group of people. The young tend to stay with the young, and the old with the old. I wish this wasn't the case because there is so much wisdom found in both places.

If you're twenty or eighty, from America or Africa, there will always be some sort of commonality. It's fascinating that we all feel like we're so different from one another that no one could possibly understand whatever we're going through. It's too easy to assume other people's lives are easier than ours, maybe it's because we don't stick around long enough to invest in whoever we envy. We aren't all that different and absolutely no one is excused from the privy of suffering. That is the human condition. We all reside in this very temporary in-between space called Earth, where we know the way this life works isn't how it's supposed to be. Struggling doesn't mean failing, that's what I keep telling myself. That is very hard for me not to believe right now. This young adult stage of life is one that you will experience, are experiencing, or have experienced, and it would be wise to learn from the people that have come before you.

Life is short, and none of us have all the time in the world to figure it out completely on our own. If we were meant to do it by ourselves, we wouldn't have such a deep longing for relationship and community. Guidance is good and necessary for growth. We nod our heads in agreement with that statement because it sounds good, but we really don't like anyone giving us advice. Most people, even if you ask for it, don't truly want it. You know what you want even if you're asking someone for their opinion; what most of us are truly in search of is validation.

To say "You do you," and "Anything goes," that right and wrong are relative to some degree, only leaves extremely impressionable people floundering. This might appease young teenagers or adults in the moment, but I wonder if, by saying that, we're doing them any favors. The reality is we all need people in our lives to help set up posts so we don't fall over the rails. No matter how much you know, you don't know it all, and once you start slipping it makes it much harder to get back up. Humans like patterns and structure; granted some of us more than others, but no one likes to feel like they're wandering around aimlessly. All of us want to know the way.

## <u>It's Just the Beginning</u>

College is built up to be the pinnacle of one's life, or at least up until that point. That it won't get any better than those four years. Phrases like, "Enjoy it while it lasts" and "These days will be the best ones of your life" are constantly spoken to us. Maybe for you college isn't the goal, but turning eighteen and starting a professional life surely is. Since we can remember, we have been preparing to get to this point and are taught how to navigate school well. As a freshman in college I looked at the seniors like they were the coolest people, and I definitely thought they had a good idea on where their lives were headed. That the "figuring it out" was for the freshmen, sophomores, and maybe even juniors, not for seniors.

Here I am, a senior in college and I do not have anything figured out. It feels like such a heavy burden that the decisions I make and the morals I place upon myself are for me to make and uphold. The way in which the rest of my life goes from here on out is on me. Then I remember it's not my job. I do not have to hold my entire life on my shoulders. My burdens, that at times feel so heavy, I can place easily on God because His are light.

As kids, most are so strictly prepared and taken care of as a student, but then after that, it's, "Okay, good luck, see you out there in the real world!" There seems to be this gap between here and there, between student and professional, child and adult, and it's deeply unsettling to be in the midst of the no longer and not yet.

### *Connect the Dots*

Here I go with the metaphors again. Life is like connect the dots, making gradual progress to eventually create a picture that just looks like a mess right now. This metaphorical game feels like there's much more at stake because I can't just erase things and pretend they didn't happen or create marks that aren't supposed to be there. I'm trying to piece together the dots from where I was to where I'm going, from who I was to who I'm becoming. That is no easy feat. Life is not linear, and progress is seldom seen as quickly as a real picture of connect the dots. Growing up in the digital age has falsified the belief that I can achieve and understand the full picture almost instantaneously. I am very quickly learning that is so far from the case, and I wish this was easier to accept than it is.

No matter where you come from or when, life is always going to be uncertain. That will never change. What can change is how you decide to live with that truth. To accept that the trajectory of your life isn't completely up to you. True strength, or at least the kind I admire, comes from knowing and accepting the limitations of ourselves and continuing on in spite of them. Although there are days when this feels impossible, I am choosing to trust a familiar God in a very unfamiliar situation. I hardly know what next week looks like, much less next year. I have seen evidence time and time again that God has gotten his people through countless times before, so there is no reason to think he would not do the same for you and me.

## <u>College Was Expected</u>

Where I'm from most people go to college, and if you don't people assume you're making the wrong decision. The look of "Are you sure you want to do that?" is definitely made toward the person considering not going. I realize this is not reality for all, but it's very much expected for the people I grew up around. College is characterized as the sweet spot in life and most people know that even if they don't personally experience it. College students party, socialize, create their own schedule for the first time, and live around all of their best friends, typically within a five-mile radius. Oh, and go to class and study. For students, graduation looms in the back of one's mind but always feels so far off.

However, as soon as my senior year started, the end became pretty clear and didn't feel so far away. It was in sight and tangible. Putting college on such a high pedestal is great for the freshmen but terrible for the seniors. Undergrad is four short years and then you move on. To put such an emphasis on a very short amount of time isn't helpful for anyone. Freshmen frequently have unrealistic expectations, while seniors feel like the peak of their life is over at the ripe age of twenty-two.

These years, in truth, were some of the best years of my life as stereotypical and cliche as that sounds. My life up until that point was not super lighthearted and carefree, and to say I struggled in middle and high school is to say almost nothing. Most days the goal during that time was to survive and stay afloat, which was not always easy going to a college preparatory school where the talent and success of the students is at such a high caliber.

I also danced competitively and if you know anything about that world it can be toxic, and I do not use that word lightly. It is extremely conniving, cut throat, and not meant for everyone, certainly not meant for me. I was in dire need of a change and that's why college changed my life and made me into a much better version of myself. I was no longer in a cookie-cutter and privileged environment where the same type of person is produced over and over again. After high school I was finally in a place where not everyone came from where I did, nor did everyone think the same way I thought. I only then began to realize how big the world is and how small I am.

So yes, for me college was great and I did not struggle much during my time there. The cliches about it being the best time of your life rang true for me, but at the same time, I understand that they are the best so far. If that was truly the pinnacle, I'm underwhelmed. I'm beginning to wonder if there even is a peak, an arrival. The people that we consider to have made it or are at the top, whatever that means, will often times speak about this and admit it's not nearly as incredible as you would think. It does not do what you thought it would, and if there was one peak we'd all be striving for the same things, but we don't. At the root of every peak is the desire to be loved, seen, and appreciated by the people that matter most to us. Rarely is an outsider's validation going to sustain your insatiable need to feel worthy. You have to decide you are.

    We can't continue to subliminally preach the message that the best years in life are four short ones in college. By doing this, we are setting graduates up to dread and fear the beginning of the rest of their lives. No one can blame us for not wanting to adult because grown-ups don't make adulting look that great a lot of the time. Why would anyone be surprised that we're hesitant about entering into it? It's going to happen to us though, growing up, so we might as well teach young people to be excited about it. Let's switch the narrative to excitement for every stage of life, not just the overly highlighted and glamorized ones.

# Chapter Two
## Transitions

When you're in the middle of them, they feel hard, confusing, and frustrating, but on the other side, it doesn't seem half as bad as it felt during the moment. Transitions are vital because they are some of the most formative moments in life, and to get to the other side is worth recognizing. They give us the opportunity to see what we're made of and test what we believe about ourselves, others, and God.

There are different types of transitions though: ones you choose and ones you don't. The ones we calculate and that coincide with our plans make believing all the good things about yourself and the world around you easier than it could be. When it's going in the opposite, it's much more challenging. Doubt sets in and before you know it you're questioning everything about yourself that you know deep down to be true.

When I reluctantly allowed myself to turn the worry and doubt about what the future holds upside down everything changed. If I can create bad scenarios in my head and convince myself it might come true, I can also wonder and dream about all of the great things that could happen as well. My imagination is one of the gifts I believe I've been given, but depending on how I channel it, two very different outcomes can occur. One paralyzes me and the other pushes me forward. Every day I pray that I will have the courage to step out in faith instead of shrink back from fear. For years my unhinged imagination was a negative thing, even at times harmful, because the ideas I created in my head caused me great amounts of distress and sometimes turned into very unhealthy behaviors. As I got older, I began to understand that I am in control of my thoughts and I can use them for good or bad. As Emily Dickinson says, "I dwell in possibility." When I look back, I see I've done that my entire life.

In my own life, and watching the lives of others around me, I have noticed that transitions seem to be a time of growth or decay. Refining and sometimes painful. Although many things in life happen to us, we do get to choose the path we go down. The little decisions and plans we make every day have an impact on how pleasant or awful our lives could become. I know that no time is wasted and my struggles, that feel amplified during this looming transition, are not for nothing. The obsessive and continual thought of 'I have no idea what I'm doing with my life' is normal for most people around my age, even though it feels like everyone else has it together more than I do.

I hate that it's so much easier to focus on the things I don't have rather than the things that I do, but that's why gratitude is essential, especially during times like this. I will not let myself forget how God has been faithful in the past and how he still is now. This redirects my heart and mind to a posture of thankfulness. No one is born grateful, and if you don't consciously pursue contentment, it will not suddenly come to you when you get what you want. Recognizing the fact that even breathing is a gift, you acknowledge everything else is extra.

## *Careers*

One of the biggest transitions of your life is when you start working. Being a young professional can be a sweet spot where the only person you have to worry about is yourself, and there aren't many times in life like that. You have the ability to focus on building something without the added pressure of having to provide for others. Creating a lasting and successful career is of the up most importance to a lot of people, myself included, but it can quickly become the ultimate thing if you let it—the only thing that matters and the sole way you deem yourself valuable. I don't want to one day years down the road realize I've let my identity get wrapped up in things I ultimately can't control. Careers, relationships, health, and money are just a few of the things we can lose.

On the contrary, who we intrinsically are has the capability to remain even if we lose everything. When we allow our happiness and joy to rely on external factors, we're constantly going to feel like we're in an unstable place, and it will only be a matter of time before you are disappointed. I care deeply about my career and the future of it, so not being able to quickly find a "career starting job" before I graduate has been hard. I constantly have to redirect my thoughts and switch my perspective to focus on the long view. I understand this is a blimp on the radar and seasons don't last forever. The tides are constantly changing just like our circumstances, and every day I remind myself that waiting isn't a curse even though it feels like it. To push back, resist, and fight this season doesn't do me any favors, and I choose to believe there's always something to be gained from the present. I just have to open my eyes to see it.

How am I going to build the career I want to? How is the life I want going to become a reality instead of a daydream that only exists in my head? I have very few answers at the moment, but refuse to fall into the trap of disqualifying myself because I'm not confident or humble enough to try. If you believe that lie long enough, you'll never do anything. Every single person on the planet is under qualified in some capacity. Guessing is a huge part of adulthood, which is something I wish wasn't true. We all have shortcomings but we also all have gifts and talents. When we recognize and cultivate these things within ourselves, by the grace of God we then get to come together and help others in ways we've been uniquely called to do. That first starts with humility.

Most days, I have to fight the lie that my life is on pause, that unless I get to where I think I should be, my life isn't meaningful right now. None of us are guaranteed tomorrow, so to not make the most of today is foolish. Finding joy in the mundane is hard, but there will always be times in everyone's life that feel unimportant and boring. You will get to the other side of whatever your current battle is, and if you're already there find people who feel stuck and encourage them. Have compassion on the people that feel like their circumstances are never going to change. When people see that word they might think kindness or something along those lines, but that's not what it is. Compassion literally means to come suffer with. Come suffer and sit with the people that are discouraged and scared. Offer your presence and a sounding voice. You might be the rock that someone desperately needs to cling to in the midst of their storm.

## *Truth*

Knowing what's true is too difficult in today's world because often times people think their opinions are the truth and nothing but. It would greatly benefit everyone if we realized that the thousands of thoughts, we have a day aren't all necessarily true.

If I believed everything that came through my head, I'd be dead a thousand times over.

During trying times it's imperative to mediate on truth and nothing else. It's scary how easily influenced we are, so if you subconsciously allow lies to seep in, you will eventually believe them. When you're in a place where you don't know what to do or where to turn, which is normal during transitions, you're even more vulnerable and impressionable than before, which makes the threshold for discernment even lower. When you don't know what you believe you'll believe anything. Recognizing this is important because you don't want to listen to everyone just because they're talking. I absolutely love to listen, read, and watch other people speak their mind, but that in no way means I take everything they say as fact.

I find truth in the one thing that has remained, the Bible, because out of all things that have come and gone, this hasn't. It's proven to be unshakeable and trustworthy, and those are the words I want to listen to. I want that kind of advice. If the Bible says small beginnings are important, they must be. The things you do and the way you talk to yourself when no one is watching, during the moments that feel less that dull, says more about who you are than anything else.

If our lives are supposed to model Jesus's think about how his life started and ended. He was born in a barn because there was no room anywhere else for his parents to deliver him, put in a feeding trough to sleep in. While on earth, He only taught and preached for three years in his adult life, and the rest of the time He was learning and growing behind the scenes. He didn't have a massive audience from the beginning and didn't come from status. The King of the world had one of the smallest starts I can think of, even though He deserved anything but. How did his life end? He rose from the dead to life after being ridiculed and killed on a cross, which is the biggest finish I can think of. Coming back to life to undeservingly save us all, proving that even death couldn't hold him down. Nothing can top that. God himself has proved that small starts are important. If Jesus's life started that modest and ended that big, I know God can do amazing things with any of our lives if we trust in his power to do so.

As I continue on my never-ending search for truth, I find myself coming back to this question. Is there a difference between knowing something and believing in it? And if so, how? The Bible, for example, I know to be true, but is it hard to believe one hundred percent of the time? Absolutely. I know that my worth doesn't come from external factors, but do I believe it all of the time? No.

Knowing feels logical, a conclusion you come to with your head. Believing something feels like it's coming from the heart, a decision based on emotion, which is why I often struggle with trusting people and things. I really don't like making decisions or forming opinions based on something I feel because, as we know, emotions a lot of the time can't be trusted. But do we have to believe in something 24/7 to know that it's true? I find that the truth is oftentimes quiet and doesn't have to scream to be heard. Sometimes knowing feels so deep it's hard to even articulate it.

# Chapter Three
# Waiting

## *Ambition and Waiting Your Turn*

One of the fundamental things we learn as children is to wait your turn. It seems simple enough, but waiting becomes harder the longer you do it. It's hard because it's never a choice we make; it happens whether we want it to or not. The essence of waiting is acceptance. The reason most people are terrible at waiting is because we cannot bear the thought that we aren't in total control of our circumstances. The more people I ask, the more I realize that we are all waiting for something; it's one of the many joys of being human. Since a great deal of life is surrounded by waiting, it would be wise to learn how to wait well. I am not good at this. Like I just mentioned, some of the key components in life, like patience, are taught at such a young age that you would think at twenty-two I would get the hang of it. Unfortunately, we all know people that never quite master the art of patience. I know I haven't, and I'm not sure any of us will fully.

I have been strong willed, determined, and very stubborn since birth. In a lot of ways, these qualities have helped me in becoming the person I want to be, but it has also made the journey that much more frustrating because sometimes it's just not my turn yet. When you have high ambition, it typically rages, so when it seems like you can't figure out how to execute a goal, it can become all-consuming. For me, this goal is to be a well-known photographer, or at least for right now, that's what seems to be the dream. I'm uncomfortable even proclaiming this aloud because it feels very lofty—too lofty, honestly.

There is no one in my personal life or outer circle that has chosen to try anything like this, so it definitely feels like the road less traveled, and at times isolating. Every single connection or job I've had relating to photography I have made or produced entirely by myself. It feels like I'm betting my life on a dream that in reality does not happen for most people in the way that I want it to. I look at other people who are seemingly so comfortable, knowing what honestly the rest of their life will look like and it can be hard not to envy that. I recently read a book by Craig Groeschel and he posed a question I now think about almost on a daily basis. He said, "What are we losing by clinging to our comfort?" Think about that.

The everyday feels slow and like I am not getting anywhere, but as long as I am the smallest bit closer to where I want to go as opposed to yesterday, that has to be good enough. Wherever you are be there—that's what I keep telling myself. I admit I self-sabotage by comparing myself to people who have been in the photography business longer than I've been alive, which clearly is only setting me up for discouragement. This sounds overt but that's what so many of us do. We compare the best and most seasoned parts of someone's life to the worst parts of our own. These legends absolutely deserve to be in that position; they've put more than their 10,000 hours in. Now the question is, what's the balance between striving and wanting more but being content and truly living?

I wish there was a perfectly balanced middle ground that could be achieved at all times, but there isn't. I romanticize the future, and for that matter, the past too, but the grass is never greener on the other side. I'm still me, and you're still you. We all have problems that monetary things or worldly recognition won't fix, and if you believe that, it's only a matter of time before you will be at the least underwhelmed, and at the worst absolutely crushed. We know this but wish it wasn't the case. I don't want to put unrealistic expectations on the prettier and flashier piece of grass and wonder why I cared so much about it in the first place.

I keep having this image of being at the top of a cliff with a huge gaping space between what's in front of me, another cliff, which is the one I feel called to. I know that's where I'm headed, but I have no idea how to get there, and any way I turn it ends up being a dead end. Never have I felt my insufficiency more than this moment and the desperate need for God to do what only he can do—make a way when there truly seems to be no way. Living in the tension of God's timing is so hard. I know what I want is his will, but I have no shame in also acknowledging what I secretly want him to do is follow my lead and hurry up.

I know God is with me here on this metaphorical cliff, what feels like the end of this particular road. Fear is persistently knocking and telling me to back down from the life I feel he's inviting me to. The one over on that other cliff which seems so impossibly out of reach. I know He's in the chasms that make no sense in the moment, and meshes the outwardly random parts of them to get us to where we are ultimately meant to be, with him. And that is enough, no matter the outcome.

In the end, it's not about lapping up all that is available and collecting things for show. Life is not a summation of the accolades and accomplishments we acquire. Recognition is great and important. Don't get me wrong; people should be appreciated for the work they do. However I cannot take anything with me when I die, so why do I care so much now? The money, status, not even our relationships. None of it is relevant in heaven. People forget everything here on Earth belongs to God and that we're only temporary managers of whatever He has chosen to bless us with. To have the long and zoomed out perspective on life can make the daily struggles a little easier.

The career path, life path really, I've chosen feels like an uphill battle because it's a competitive space, but most everything is if you let yourself think that way. To make it big in a creative industry is undeniably hard. I'm in the midst learning that I don't have to been in the top one percent to be a valuable asset in society. I don't have to be the very best at something to be really great at it. I'm learning how to be, not do.

When we focus only on doing, it's too easy to put your entire identity in that. The problem there is that it's fleeting, whatever you're doing, and you're allowing your well-being to be at the mercy of other people and their decisions. I cannot live like that. I do not want to one day be sitting alone, wondering who I am and how to just be, and can't. Sure, I want people to know my name. I want to make it, but when I really try to define what that means or why I feel that way, it's hard to do.

We hear that phrase constantly and don't think much about it, "making it." I didn't until recently. To me, it means to have success in one area or another, but even better if it's in multiple areas. That feeling is something we all crave since before we even have the language for it. I began to wonder if the people I consider to have made it, if they feel like they have too. Are they content with their lives? Because if I had theirs, surely, I'd feel great about it.

Our culture has gotten it sorely wrong that to be deemed important, special, or significant you have to do something extraordinary with your life. Thousands, even better millions, need to know about it. Extraordinary and significant are very subjective, just like success is, so if you don't define what that means to you, good luck reaching it. Some of the people I acclaim to be the most successful are the ones who have realized their own value and have delayed gratification in a significant way. And no, I do not consider someone to be successful just because they have money or a huge social media following. They do not have a better ranking in society because of that. The sooner we realize that the better off we will be.

How does that phrase benefit us, "making it." I would imagine once someone feels they've reached that point, they might stop striving. Maybe even settle for where they are because they feel they can't grow any more. If we set pride aside and take a hard look at our life, I wonder if the outcomes would stay the same. I think a lot of us are settling. Too many choose to stay with what we've always known because it's familiar. We don't want to risk the potential of the unknown even if it could lead to something so much better than what you already have. I don't want to put myself, my career, my relationships in a box because I think I know what's best. I don't. There's always room to learn and grow.

One of the many results of staying with what's familiar is burn out, which is at an all-time high. So much so that even teenagers feel it. Too much of a good thing typically turns sour. The hard part about implementing balance in any area of life, is that it is considered completely normal to way outdo, overachieve, and run oneself to total depletion. We incessantly praise the people that never stop to rest, as if that somehow makes them better.

We can't do anything effectively if we're exhausted. We all know this but why do we still do it? If you don't have a full-time job, a side hustle, hobbies, and a very busy social life, you might be lazy. Before people turn thirty, they're sick of their jobs because they've let it utterly consume them. Work is important but it doesn't define us. The way we subconsciously rank people by how much they do and make is bizarre.

Without realizing it, older adults have set examples that if you aren't grinding 24/7, you aren't doing enough. And because of that you aren't enough. Teenagers and young people naturally follow their lead because we think they know what they're doing. We assume they know better. We think if our small business hasn't turned into a multimillion-dollar company within a few years, it might be time to throw in the towel. That is slightly dramatic, and maybe you're reading this and think I sound crazy, I definitely could be. But this is how it feels and I know I can't be the only one. Normally, people only talk about the process after they've achieved said success. No one really seems to care about all of the hard work that happened before, but then wonder why they feel like a failure when things don't seem to happen quickly enough for themselves.

As I watch other people's successes unfold, it becomes increasingly difficult for me to not feel like I'm falling behind. It seems like everyone else is having their moment when mine has not even begun to take shape. Other people's success does not deter my own. I genuinely remind myself of this daily, and when I don't, I so quickly become enveloped by bitterness.

Up until now, my peers and their lives have been somewhat comparable to mine because all we've ever done is school. Yes, we could get jealous of someone's clothes or body, but when you grow up a little, you realize that's all largely insignificant. Now, though? We're comparing and watching to see how we emerge into the real world. That's a lot different of a comparison than before.

For my own benefit, I know I need to focus on my own life and how to improve it before I wish for someone else's, but everyone else's is constantly in my face. When I start to feel like my life isn't cool enough to share, not even with close friends, I ask myself who am I trying to impress? Who am I trying to make it for? The brutal truth is everyone is much too concerned about themselves to be watching if you're "making it." No one cares if you are because they're only focused on if they will.

When you choose to have an audience of one, it makes life much easier. Grace rewrites our stories every single time—that's the beautiful thing about leaving your value up to God. You don't have to do anything to attain it. Stepping into the person you've always been destined to be often feels like stepping into the great unknown. I deeply understand that and am right there too. Good things, often times God things, take lots of time. A famous quote by the Japanese theologian Kosuke Koyama claims, "The speed of God is three miles per hour." That feels right to me.

Stop deeming what's cool based on the ever-changing trends because the world will always tell you you're not good enough, cool enough, and the only way to stay relevant enough is to appease your audience with whatever the popular opinion is. And if not, you'll be unimportant, forgotten, and probably cancelled. But the truth is, as C.S. Lewis poses, "You will never make a good impression on other people until you stop thinking about what sort of impression you are making."

Why have so many of us gotten it in our heads that to have a significant influence on others, you have to live in a cool city (the bigger the better), dress in a trendy way (the more expensive the piece, the better), and post a ridiculous amount of Instagram story updates on what you are doing. Not to mention, just because you have influence doesn't mean you'll have an impact. You're not going to wondrously become the person you want to be when you have an audience. More than likely, an audience will make it much harder for you to be who you genuinely are. I learned this not by hearing anyone else talk about it or by one day randomly believing I have influence; I learned it from babysitting.

    Growing up, I had incredible babysitters. This job might seem monotonous and potentially insignificant, but it definitely isn't. You know the age when a cool teenager comes over with their own car, drives you around, and talks to you like they are your best friend. They seem so old and sure of themselves and are the most fun. They made me feel cool, seen, and important. My sister and I became so obsessed with one of the girls, that we made T-shirts with her name on them. We painted "I Heart Jessica Club" in huge letters and showed up to dance one day wearing them for her to see. At the time truly no one was cooler, and because of not only her but the other examples I had, I knew the kind of babysitter I wanted to be one day.

    Fast forward years later, in college I worked with a family that made my experience even better than I thought it could be. I spent a few years with them and took great initiative to be the best example I could for these girls because I knew it mattered. I wanted to be the cool babysitter I had for them. If you want to know what you believe and what is important to you take notice of the way you act and where you spend your time—that's the best indicator life can give you. I learned how great my influence was on two girls by playing and talking with them day in and day out. I learned this by investing in their real lives, not by having two million followers on Instagram who I don't know, and preaching one-minute sound bites to hopefully go viral.

## *Celebrities*

I find celebrities absolutely fascinating and not in the way most people do. I've never really had a celebrity crush and honestly am more enamored with how massively influenced and obsessed people are with them. Well that's kind of a lie; I love the Jennifer's in Hollywood, besides them I don't care too much. I was born and raised in Nashville so fame didn't seem like such a foreign thing. I never thought twice about my aunt being good friends with Dierks Bentley, and when she died, he sang at her bedside. Or the time at the dentist when I walked into the waiting room to find Nicole Kidman and Keith Urban. Or when I saw Reba at Pottery Barn. Growing up in Nashville it's understood you leave them alone because this is their home. When you see these people in everyday life you understand they aren't any different than you and me. They go to the dentist and they go to Pottery Barn. The way many people view celebrities is borderline inhumane. As Jon Tyson says, "We live in a world where people are viewed as commodities. In our culture, people don't offer goods and services. They become the goods and services."

Don't get me wrong, I'm often inspired and in awe of the talent a lot of them possess. The work ethic, ambition, and grit that you find in and surrounding that industry is outstanding and seldom unmatched. That is what I find inspiring. They're just people with feelings and emotions, and the things that make our lives hard make theirs hard too. They get sick, sad, jealous, insecure—all of it. Shocking! Of course this is all speculation, but I'd even go as far to say that some struggle to a greater degree because of how many eyes are on them. How much harder that must be to truly find out what you're passionate about when people believe the summation of who you are is what you do and what you put out for millions to see? I cannot fathom what that is like.

In America, which is often characterized as an individualistic and power-hungry society, it's a very common believe that the more you have the happier you'll be. When is it enough? Apparently never, unless you make the conscious effort to believe that it is. We all have a massive void only God can fill. The amount of praise and adoration we bestow upon celebrities was never meant for them, and I think this is a reason so many struggle to such an extreme degree. It's so abnormal how many people follow, keep up with, and judge every single move they make. I imagine some of them know this too well; you might be seen by millions but known by none, or very few. Or the feeling, as John Steinbeck puts it, "I wonder how many people I've looked at all my life and never seen." We look at people in the public eye and objectify them so much, but do we see them? My guess is no, and to a degree, we shouldn't. We all should have the right to privacy and just because one part of someone's life is forward-facing does not mean the people consuming it deserve exclusive access to the entirety of their lives. That would be ridiculous! But that's what we as the consumers expect. Since you are in movies, you must tell us about your marriage and fertility journey. We all agree with this, but we don't act like we do. I heard an incredible quote years ago, I wish I could remember who said it, and it has stuck with me ever since: "The only thing money can buy is bubble wrap." Unfortunately, no one is excluded from the hardships of life, it just might make the blow a little softer.

I wonder if once everyone knows their names, they wish at times people didn't. I can't help but think if we treated celebrities like the humans they are, this huge gap between "normal and famous" would decrease a lot. Why do you think "normal people" feel bad about themselves when they see celebrities making millions, traveling around the world, and looking perfect while doing it? We only see the success, the payoff. We did not see the hard work, dedication, doubt, insecurity, rejection, and failure that most definitely preceded those shiny moments. Life isn't as dreamy as it looks on Instagram. They're just people trying to find their place like you and me, and at times I imagine it's even harder for them, trying to find themselves, because there is such an expectation. An image and an agenda that people demand from them, and if they don't deliver? On to the next.

Feeling like you have nothing to lose and everything to gain can obviously feel sad because by saying that, you're also insinuating that currently you have nothing, or very little. To some degree that is where I am at so I can attest to these feelings, but it might be a blessing in disguise. We see all of the good parts of having a very public influence but if we knew everything, the reality of that world and how unglamorous it can be, I don't think as many people would want it.

### *Easy Access*

It isn't completely uncommon to see people become famous overnight. One TikTok goes viral and suddenly a person's entire life is changed. It isn't unusual to see celebrities have decade's worth of wild success and then wrongly assume the road to that was somewhat quick and easy. We can see virtually anything we want to in seconds, and it's undeniable that it's given all of us a false sense of reality. We will never be able to know and see everything, but because of the internet, we think we can. Building a purposeful life takes a lot of time. The internet does not reflect real life and cannot accurately depict the depth and nuance from one person to the next, but our lives do revolve around the media. That makes figuring things out, what's real and what's not, how life really works and how it doesn't, very hazy.

I don't want to undermine these outline-type stories, where a person's success is accomplished very quickly and somewhat randomly, however, most stories are not written that way. This has falsely influenced my believe system that if something is harder than I thought it would be, or not working out within the time frame I've deemed acceptable, then it must not be right. I second-guess myself when whatever it is takes longer than I think it should. The specific path life takes each one of us down will never be completely clear. I wish so badly there was a map on where to go and how to get there the quickest and most pain-free way, but there isn't. God promises a light, headlights really, so we can see what's right in front of us, which is all we need. He doesn't give us all the details because they aren't necessary. Stop trying to see two hundred miles down the road and focus on the two right in front of you.

I don't want to miss out on the blessings below my nose because I'm squinting trying to see what's so far out. In times when it seems like nothing is going my way, I'm choosing to trust that God will see me through the vision I believe he has called onto my life. I can't imagine He's gotten me, us, this far just to get us this far. Why would he do that? He's too good of a God to leave us hanging.

## *Afraid to Make the Wrong Move*

Isn't it strange that at eighteen years old kids are supposed to have a pretty good idea about what they want to do with the rest of their life? Feeling pressed to make decisions that could affect the rest of your life at eighteen can create debilitating anxiety, and in turn, makes it very hard to make any kind of decision.

We become so afraid to make the wrong move that we don't make any. Some of us are afraid to disappoint people or maybe even God, but he isn't a genie and does not have our every move planned out to a tee. We have free will. God does not have one narrow path that everyone needs to follow, and if you step off of it, you definitely are not done for. He isn't controlling, and we aren't robots despite what you might have been told.

God is not looking down waiting to punish, or delighted to punish you when you mess up, which you will. Or maybe you think you're too far gone to even care what he thinks. Don't give yourself that much credit, you aren't that powerful. Despite what you may believe, God wants his children to have and benefit from good things. Grace, mercy, and love are his natural tendencies because that is who he is. This is hard to comprehend because we naturally love up until a certain point and live in a world where love is predominately conditional. We love until they do us wrong or until they offend us. Perfect love, God's love, does not work like that. There is no pit too deep that God's love can't drown, and your specific wrongdoings are nothing God hasn't worked with or seen before. So make the big moves and trust that God is going to work all of them together for the good even when you misstep.

# Chapter Four
# Google

I love Google, sometimes a little too much. Don't we all? Checking is my biggest OCD habit whenever I am anxious. I might Google something ten times to make sure I find every possible answer, even though I know in the span of ten minutes, there is no new information. I know this won't help me in the long run but it is so hard to deny myself. It's much better, my checking habits, but there are still times when I succumb and cave to extensive and very unnecessary research. Naturally, whenever I'm curious about something, I turn to Google, so I decided to see what I could find about growing up and how the internet defines adulthood. One particular article by Psychology Today did grab my attention because of its somewhat obvious practicality.

Like I've previously mentioned, I'm very curious by nature and tend to question everything and everyone. I am not quick to trust and I'm definitely skeptical—sometimes cynical if I let myself go. I appreciate my analytical brain, but I would be lying if I said it didn't majorly contribute to my anxiety. The more you know, the scarier the world is. Ignorance does tend to be blissful.

I googled: Is adulthood really just an age? Is it a feeling, success, money, or power? Or is it defined differently depending on the person you ask? I have found myself constantly grasping for concrete markers of adulthood, but have come to the unfortunate realization that there isn't one thing, one feeling, or one moment that says you've gotten there. Growing is much more complicated than a check list. Some of the bolded titles you see listed below are bullet points from this article on definers of adulthood.

## *Don't Be A Jerk*

Simple enough? You would think, but it can be extremely hard to do sometimes. We've all been a jerk and will be again. It's funny to remember that as children we often scream, cry, and meltdown over something as biological as hunger or fatigue. Or how when children are annoyed or mad at a friend, they tell them without beating around the bush. They haven't learned how to filter their thoughts and emotions so they don't. It frustrates me that adults have to hold it together all of the time. Or do we?

As we age, it seems that emotions are not something to show or express, but to hide. Or at least dilute so they don't make others uncomfortable. Or to shove them down until we can't take it anymore. We then end up having a meltdown just like we did when we were five but this time, it's probably behind closed doors when no one can see it. Bottling things up isn't the answer, (which is what I tend to do) even though it's easier in the moment. We tell kids to suck it up, don't cry. That crying is for babies, but then, when they grow up into adults, we wonder why they can't properly express emotions and have mature conversations.

Obviously, it would be ridiculous and inappropriate for adults to scream in long lines because they weren't moving. Tantrums aren't the way to healthily express frustration, I think we can all agree on that much. With that though, children can offer so much insight and wisdom that we often times don't pay attention to, and we should take the raw and honest emotions that children naturally express and carry that over into our adult lives.

The lack of varying emotions in many adults is something I have taken notice of, and naturally has made me wonder why. We are all just "fine." Why is it so hard to be honest if someone asks how I'm doing? Why is it so hard to say I am not okay? We can't pick and choose emotions; they're all a package deal when we're born. I pushed back on this so much as a child, I still do, but I know it's physically, mentally, and spiritually healthier to express them all rather than pretend I don't deal with certain ones. Depending on the person, certain emotions are definitely easier to express than others. That's normal, but to pretend you're not an emotional person is extremely aloof, and I can say that because that is me. I do not like to be moved emotionally; I'd rather be moved logically, but life doesn't really work that way. We can't fully live unless you radically accept that being a human is extremely emotional. I have a really hard time with that.

Why do emotions feel so personal and private when that's one of the only things we have common? We all deal with them, so what's the big deal in showing it. When people come together and bring light to what they feel, freedom is found, and compassion rises. We might not be as big of jerks if we leaned into this.

Another phenomenon that strikes me is the saying, "If you want to know the truth, ask a kid." Don't you think it should be, if you want to know the truth, ask an adult? Shouldn't we know more? Shouldn't we be wiser? Kids tell it like it is and it's great, hilarious, and cute. When adults do it, it can be funny, but more times than not it is rude, unwarranted, and weird. Believe me I know. I am very blunt and some people don't like it. As I continue to grow, I have to think about the best way to get something across to ensure I don't sound like a jerk. Now, yes, this is a mature thought and not a bad thing to do at all, to filter what you say, but I ultimately believe that most of us think this way because we don't want anyone to feel anything except happy, good, or comfortable. I don't want to be a prick, but I also don't think it's my responsibility to ensure your comfort at all times. Sometimes the truth just hurts. There's no way around it. Exercise is good for you but is it comfortable? No. That's the way I often times look at truth. We have to have people in our lives that keep us accountable because how are any of us supposed to grow from or learn anything if we don't?

Emotions are good and when we don't address them that's when we tend to act like jerks. Honesty and clarity make life much easier. Everyone is better off if we treat others with kindness. Notice I didn't say niceness. I believe kind people are genuine and have the best interest of the person in mind. Niceness feels surface level. Kindness is much deeper than that.

## *Responsibility Equals Freedom*

Eleanor Roosevelt says it best, "Freedom makes a huge requirement of every human being. With freedom comes responsibility. For the person who is unwilling to grow up, the person who does not want to carry his own weight, this is a frightening prospect." A cornerstone for adulthood is maturation, and with that, freedom.

Responsibility is one thing that frightens young adults because it feels like a lot of weight to carry. Does the weight of responsibility ever go away or do you just get used to it? As young people, for our entire lives so far, most of us have leaned on our own parents or parental figures for basic needs, advice, and excuses if we are honest. I have a few stories about how I learned that I'm at the age where I can't blame things on my parents or anyone else. What I do now is up to me. The choices I make are on me and me alone. My parents can't and shouldn't save the day.

I can remember two instances when I understood responsibility, and they definitely make me laugh, so feel free to laugh at me too. As we all know, college or moving out of the house quickly makes you realize all of the luxuries you once had at your fingertips, it did for me. First, you need to know both of my parents are pharmacists, and a classic trait of theirs can be overly organized and clean. Because of this, I lived in a very neat and tidy house. My sister and I joke that unless we're at our home in Nashville, we're never fully clean because no place is cleaner than the house we grew up in. As I navigated the first weeks of college, I remember having the thought of, if I want to live in a clean place, I have to clean it. If I want to eat good food, I have to cook. Before, I always had an abundance of delicious food and lived in a very clean environment but now, if I wanted that, I had to do it for myself. I must mention I fully understand and see the privilege I had as a child. Coming from a loving home with parents and grandparents that wanted to do everything for me is something I do not take for granted in the slightest.

The second responsibility realization happened to me at a photoshoot when I was about twenty. I shot for a small country singer, which was one of my first jobs with a full crew, talent, directors, and makeup artists, etcetera. Stakes felt high, especially because I was at least ten years younger than everyone else on set. Something about the entertainment industry that everyone might not know is that there is usually no true set end time. I learned that very quickly and still am not used to it. Shoots last as long as they need to last. I love sleep, though, and require a lot of it. So, on this particular evening, when the time kept ticking longer and longer than I thought it would, I had the thought, "Oh! I can just go tell the director my parents want me home by 11." That's hilarious and ridiculous. As a kid my parents would often say, blame it on us, we don't care. I took full advantage of that and wish I still could. This was a situation where if I was younger, that would be totally valid, but standing there in a cabin shooting with one of my first clients; I actually wanted to blame my parents for wanting to leave early because of the overtime. Nice one, Abby.

## *Love Hard and Responsibly*

Woah. To start, you need to know a little bit more about me. I'm through and through a no-bullshit type of person, and for whatever reason, the tender and sweet emotions sometimes feel too vulnerable, almost embarrassing. It's always felt easier to keep a wall up than to let it down and potentially get hurt. Loving someone at times feels naive, like trusting your own judgment and their character to be who they say they are, and then allowing yourself to believe it. That's intense.

It's not that I don't crave relationship and love people, but trust is everything when it comes to deep connection. Trust is surrender, and surrender is so incredibly hard. To love is to sacrifice, it's giving up part of you and showing up for the other even when you don't want to. So many people, especially young ones, partake in a selfish kind of love. They think their significant other is theirs for the taking and the first thing they think of when it comes to love is receiving it, not giving it. They think if their significant other isn't meeting every single one of their needs all of the time, they aren't doing a good enough job. True love is selfless, not something to try and take as much as you can get. Real love is very costly. It's generous and that's one of the many reasons it's so hard. How much are you willing to lose for the sake of someone else? That is mature love, and really the only kind I am interested in.

I can't help but think about how the people that I love are always going to be coming and going. I kind of hate that. Whether that is, "I'll see you in a few weeks, or I'll see you again in heaven." When I think about that, it makes my stomach drop to the floor. The unhealthy part of me wants to pull away and pretend like I don't want or need family and friends. Other times, I tend to fall on the other extreme and want to be with them whenever possible because I know they won't always be here. I feel like I need to do everything with them because I know one day the option won't be there. I also know I can't put my own life on hold to be in every part of my families. On the romantic side of things, well, I tend to avoid that.

Here's a little more that you need to know to understand the fuller picture. I grew up with one younger sister, Claire, but we were raised as twins. We would be millionaires if we had a dollar for every time people asked us that growing up. We're just eighteen months apart and she's in the grade directly under me, so we shared the same friends and did the same things. Not because we were forced to but we liked to be around the same people, share the same humor, and have genuinely always enjoyed each other's company.

We grew up in a dance studio and the circles we ran in never included boys. We were definitely not the girls who were boy-obsessed in middle or high school, and the friends we had were typically like-minded. People dated, but not as much as you would expect from high schoolers. Where we spent middle and high school was a very egocentric place focused on furthering yourself, so for most, relationships weren't at the top of everyone's priority. And, honestly, I thought the girls that could only think and talk about boys were boring and sad. Interestingly though, I've noticed that no matter what, most of the time, if there's a room full of girls they almost always end up talking about boys, this still rings true today. For whatever reason the conversation always seems to goes there. Why?

I always pushed the thoughts about romantic relationship out of my head, saying, "Oh, I'll just find someone in college." Well, here I am in college, actually one semester from graduating, and I'm definitely not in a position where I want to be in serious relationship. It feels wrong that I don't want that right now, and where I come from definitely has a part in my thinking this way. I'm from the conservative south, right in the middle of the Bible Belt, so getting married young and having children is at the top of the priority list for most. Because of this, it can feel like I'm behind in that regard when in reality I know I'm not. I will not buy into the lie that my life is missing something because I don't have this one thing, and I'm not going to search for cheap relational encounters just because now seems to be the age where people want to do so.

If or when I decide to commit to a person it will not be because I've always wanted to be married. I frankly don't care about the successful husband, the white picket fence, the 2.5 kids, and the golden retriever in the beautifully cut front lawn. I've never had a wedding Pinterest board, definitely do not have a list of baby names in my phone, and I honestly haven't seen an engagement ring that I don't think could also be from Target. I will not get into any relationship just because I can't possibly imagine being single for the rest of my life. Because I can and it doesn't scare me. It will be solely because of him. It will be because he is worth sacrificing the life I have, the one that I love, to build one even greater together.

Do I want to eventually fall in love and marry one day? Probably, but as a twenty-two-year-old, the thought of loving someone at such an intimate level is just not what I want to focus on. I have the rest of my life to do that. I will say though, love is such a force, and the longer I push it away in this form, the scarier it seems. It's heartbreaking that people fall so hard and end up with nothing but a broken heart. I've seen it enough times to know how sad it is. It's so maddening to me that this type of relationship can bring such destruction to someone, so much so that sometimes a person will think their life is over because of it.

I have no problem admitting I'm selfish right now and I'm sure you can see that. If there was ever a time to be so, it would be now. I'm not going to let myself feel like the oddball because I want something different. It's okay for me to not want a serious relationship because I am twenty-two, and it would be fine if I was sixty-two and still didn't want it. Why do people automatically assume if you're single you didn't choose it? Wake up. It's not 1950. What's good for you might not be for someone else. Why does it feel like the pinnacle of a woman's life is to get married and have children, dare I say like you aren't complete until you do so? I'm frustrated because those questions are valid, but there is also a part of me that wishes I could relax, go on casual dates, and not think about all of these things, but alas.

Any time I open Instagram someone new has a significant other, is engaged, or is pregnant. Suddenly, there are people that have never had boyfriends before, getting into very serious relationships. Does this make me excited for the future? Sure, but

I feel bad for saying it makes me sad too. I'm that incredibly weird person that goes to weddings and is somewhat sad about it. Yes, there's new life and love to be celebrated, but you're also saying goodbye to a time and a family that won't ever look the same again. I sometimes wish we could all be innocent kids not worrying about whether or not we'll get married or have our own kids, wondering when or if that time will ever come. I wish we could still be the girls that don't have deep wounds from past relationships, scars that may never fully go away. I want my friends and my sister to confide in me first and not their significant other. It can feel like I'm losing friends because of guys and it's sad. They say nothing will change but it will, there's no way for it not to. I know this isn't entirely logical, but we all know those people that once they got into a relationship your friendship with them becomes nonexistent. I know I'm not losing anyone just because there's an addition, but if I do that means that person wasn't meant to be in my life forever, which is okay. For the most part I like change and handle it well, or at least I thought I did. Relational changes are hard for me to accept because they are changes that last forever. People, especially ones that you love, don't leave you neutral. I am too aware of this.

## *My Life Versus My Families*

I never thought about my own individual life too much until I went to college. I always identified with my family as a unit, I am them and they are me. That might sound cute and I guess it is, but because of this, fully coming into my own person and creating my own life aside from my families feels unnatural and at times wrong. Realizing I'm an extension of them, not them, is something I haven't really given much thought until now.

So many people live in the shadow of their families or their past, but I don't want to do that. I am eternally grateful that I did not have parents that put pressure on me to be a certain type of person. I never once felt the need to be someone I'm not. I wonder how many people, probably unconsciously, have kids to have a second chance, a redo of the childhood they wish they had. It is very obvious that some parents live through their kids, and I'm so glad those were not mine. Although I feel no pressure from them to be successful, there is a part of all of us that wants to please our parents, especially when you're young. I don't struggle with the anxiety of pleasing them, hoping to get their approval, I know I have that no matter what I do. I do struggle with occasional guilt for feeling like I'm leaving them behind. They gave me life and I'm just leaving them high and dry? Thanks for my childhood, bye. Having monumental realizations and experiences that do not include them feels somewhat dishonorable and sad to me. Why? Parents don't have babies to have babies forever. The goal has always been for them to turn into independent, kind, and loving, successful people in whatever capacity is achievable for them. It's time for me to fully step into that reality.

### *Stop Lying*

There's not much to say about it except don't do it. We learn from the moment we can understand what lying is to not. Lying is so easy when you're a child, well; actually it is for a lot of adults too. Our conscious should develop as we age which allows us to understand the consequences and detrimental effects of lying.

Truth always prevails and will come out eventually. I have been called too honest plenty of times but I take it as a compliment. I don't think too honest should be a thing.

## *Check Your Ego*

There will always be egotistical people in the world. We know at least one but probably more than that. Some of that behavior is learned but a lot of it is acquired. Being from a wealthy and sheltered bubble of Nashville I know my fair share of conceited people. I'm not knocking where I come from at all, but the reality of how I grew up can easily breed this type of person. As a kid, it tends to be all about "Me, me, me." One of the first words we learn is "mine." Most kids are egocentric because they can't even slightly understand selflessness and the power of humility. I see and understand how easy it can be to be self-absorbed, especially when you have been handed a nice deck of cards. I also understand that if you are self-made and have paved a successful path from nothing, in turn you believe you've earned your wealth and recognition. That you're successful solely because of your own two hands. Egos are the biggest turn off, and I personally only want to follow humble people. No one likes conceitedness. If you have nice things you feel like you deserve it, but the world doesn't owe you anything.

True fulfillment is found in giving and the smallest amount of generosity goes so far. Even if you aren't aware of this, if you experience it, you can't help but want to do that for someone else. Why do you think we are moved to tears when we see or partake in acts of kindness? No one is moved to tears by thinking about themselves. True success and power should be measured by how we give to others freely without expecting anything in return.

We're hardwired to serve. The reason most of us choose the career we do is to help others in some way. Maybe that wasn't the original intention, but after a while, that's what it becomes. Wouldn't you be heartbroken if at the end of your life someone told you that you could've done so much more if only your ego didn't get the way? The reality is if there was a person who visited everyone before they die and gave them a report; I think a lot of people would receive that news. Life isn't about what we do but how and why we do it. It's about the way we treat people in the messiness of our lives. Gandhi proclaims, "When the ego dies, the soul awakes."

## *Call People Back*

One of my biggest pet peeves is when people don't text me back in an appropriate amount of time. I know you're on your phone and see my text. I of course forget to text people back and sometimes don't want to respond immediately. There's plenty of grace for that. It's important to have time without technology, but for the most part we always have our phones near or on us at all times. It's rude not to respond in a timely manner, and it's common courtesy to respond to people. I know this advice is to call people back, but texting applies as well. I'm deeply sorry that I'm an annoying Gen-Z, but I don't love phone calls and they used to make me really anxious. I'd much rather text. Not so much the actual act of talking on the phone, but what could go down during is what freaks me out.

At the height of this specific worry, something that would immediately spike my heart rate was when one of my family members would call me without warning first. Really if anyone called me I wasn't expecting, it scared me. My brain went to the worst-case scenario almost every time the phone rang because for the longest time I associated phone calls with bad news. Even though it's much better, my stomach flips a little when my phone rings. I've watched horrifying phone calls come through the phone so I unfortunately associate the two.

Now as an adult I obviously can't avoid phone calls, so to help me overcome this irrational fear my therapist made people randomly call me to talk about nothing. To decrease the spike of anxiety I felt when my phone rang. It was annoying but it helped; exposure therapy is terrible and amazing. Anyway, texting, calling, or emailing in an appropriate time frame is adults.

## *Take Care of Your Own Stuff*

Straightforward and to the point, self-explanatory but vital. I had to learn this quickly because both of my parents have worked full time my entire life. They couldn't just bring something to us at the drop of a dime if we forgot it because they had their own work and schedules to abide by. I'm not someone who loses things often, mainly because I don't love stuff and don't have a ton of it, but knowing my parents couldn't come bring me something just because I wasn't prepared made me more aware of my own things, maybe earlier than some kids learn.

## *Be Grateful*

Gratitude is accompanied by awareness which is something children typically lack. A lot of adult's lack awareness too. I wish the two were as synonymous as they should be. As we age, we realize we live in dark world and that bad things unfairly happen all of the time. Our attitude and outlook is one of the few things we have control over in this life. To see the bad in this world is so easy; you don't have to seek it out, it's just there. To look for the good? That takes practice, courage, and perspective. It's been proven time and time again that gratitude changes things, something I try to implement in my every day.

I don't want to one day, decades from now, realize all of the great things I had in my life. There's always going to be something I don't have that someone else does. That's just the way life works. It's easier to sit in the discontentment of the things we hope for instead of choosing joy in the midst of what feels like lack.

# Chapter Five
# Senior Year and My Chaotic Thoughts

*It's Happening*

It's not this far-off thing happening in a year, a few months, or even in a few weeks. It's now, and it feels like so many of the decisions I've made up until this point are about to come to a head. Am I going to be able to accomplish the things I want to? Did I make the right career choice? Whenever I started to worry about these things in college I could always brush it off because I was still in school. There's only so much you can do to further a career when you're a full-time student and have a schedule you have to abide by. In two weeks I'll be a college graduate. Before now I thought by the time the end of my senior year came, I would have a slight idea about what was next. Was I naive in thinking this? Probably, but if you ask a senior in high school how you expect a senior in college to feel, I can almost guarantee they would not say, "I bet some of them have no idea what they're doing and are totally freaking out." Unless you have been through that experience, the narrative is that we have a pretty good idea on what we're, college seniors, doing with our lives. I thought pieces of my puzzle would've come together by now.

    I'd be lying to you if I said I never touted myself on knowing what I want and having my ducks in a row most of the time. I'm naturally very decisive and never understood how some are okay with no plan. I tend to live this quote, "If you fail to plan, you plan to fail." I wrongly assumed that meant whoever didn't have a detailed plan also didn't have driven or a vision for their life. Boy was I wrong, and because of that, this season has been incredibly humbling in more ways than one. I do not know what I'm doing. I'm scared, unsure, and wish I would have been more honest about this with myself prior to a few days before I graduate. I think I subconsciously believed the portrayal that when people say "I don't know what I'm doing," that means they have not one ounce of an idea on where to turn, but if someone does "Have it figured out," then they have absolutely one hundred percent of everything figured out. Neither of these extremes are true, normal, or common. No one can hold it together and know all the things we need to all of the time.

It boils down to imposter syndrome. This topic has been widely talked about frequently in the past few years because people are finally putting words to something that everyone feels—an internal belief that you are not as competent as the others around you. Why does it feel like everyone around me knows what they're doing but I don't? I wish I didn't struggle with this but I do more often than I would like to admit.

I assume the demographic that struggles with this the most is young adults, but I know it excludes no one. I wonder if part of the issue is not being honest with how we're really doing—too many act fine in public but are a wreck in private. Would imposter syndrome decrease if we were even slightly more transparent with others? Not to mention the loneliness pandemic is through the roof even though we're the most "connected" we've ever been. I can't help but think if we addressed how we really are with transparency, imposter syndrome would decrease and lead to deeper relationships; which is what all of us really want.

## *Graduation*

I am not looking forward to this. I'm proud of myself and thankful to be in this position, but what ensues after I walk across the stage, I am slightly terrified of. With such a big end in sight, I'm trying to learn how to hold both sadness and joy in the same hand without becoming inundated in one or the other. During the fall semester, I thought I wasn't nervous for what's to come. I knew I was on the way to something that was unknown, but it truthfully didn't make me that nervous. Everyone surrounding me was in the same position, so I didn't feel alone. This wasn't an act. I did feel this way, but I definitely tried to play it cool a little too much. Now I'm just a few short weeks from this all being over, and I'm finally telling myself it's okay to be nervous. I wish I was more honest with myself then because now my anxiety is higher than I expected it to be.

My career is seldom an anxiety trigger for me and I've rarely doubted myself in this way. (I'm laughing out loud as I edit this a year later. That could not be further from the truth now… I'll explain later.) I know my self-worth has nothing to do with my external circumstances but it doesn't feel like it. The world tells us the things we accomplish, the physical evidence of it, is when merit is deserved. I've applied to countless jobs and the only thing I hear back is "I'm sorry but we are going in a different direction," or "Your application is still under review," or it's never looked at. As you can imagine this really boosts self-confidence. It becomes easier to believe the lies that come into my head as each day passes. Lies like "I'm not qualified," and "No one sees me," become validated.

I know my burdens, worries, hardships, and every other feeling I have is what qualifies me to go to God and ask for help.

This is often when he does his best work, when his children realize they need Him. He doesn't expect or want me to come to him in a glorified put together persona because he knows I am not that. No one is, and the things I struggle with don't make me a liability to God. He knows my every thought so I might as well go to him with how I really feel. The best part is you don't have to think about filtering what you say which is a huge plus for me since I have such a hard time doing that anyway.

We can trust in what he's doing and know he understands, because he first endured the most extreme amount of pain and loss possible. Even Jesus experienced rejection. If we really knew the heart of Jesus, not what culture has labeled Christianity, nothing would stop us from going to him in every moment. On a podcast this week, someone said this, and I cannot stop thinking about it. "Christianity can be extremely confusing, but Jesus is wildly compelling." That is one of the truest statements I've heard in a long time. Find out for yourself who God really is, not what mainstream culture depicts Christianity to be. You owe it yourself to ask the big questions.

A lot of us, if we're really honest with ourselves, are maybe afraid of God. I definitely have been. It's valid to, at times, be fearful of the God who created the universe and everything else, because it's not comprehendible to fully know how big He is. Don't feel bad about feeling this way; doubting and questioning is good. God can handle it. The unfortunate yet undeniable truth is the way Christians act is not always a true representation of Christ, actually a fair amount of the time it probably isn't. Our world has sorely twisted what it means to find and follow Jesus.

What I will not let myself forget is that God is constantly at work by providing and protecting things, for me and you, that we can't possibly know about yet. He's created a way for my ultimate good that I couldn't conjure up even on my best day. He goes so far before us that to worry about the small nuanced details of everyday life is futile, but way easier said than done.

On the off chance, if you're unaware of the fact that there are countless things to worry about, I'm here to tell you. Millions of things can go wrong at any given moment and it's a wonder anyone goes out and does anything. Although logic and reason rarely appease anxiety, it does not logically make sense to worry about one thing—you might as well worry about it all. To pick and choose what's risky based on your own life experience does not make a lot of sense. What's "safe" is an illusion. We do have another option—to not worry about any of it. To lead a daring and bold life which I don't think includes worry, doubt, shame, or fear.

### *Journaling*

A cliché people like to post about: waking up before sunrise to post a picture of their coffee and journal onto their Instagram stories. I used to think journaling was pointless and had no idea what these self-made journalists were writing about. Until you do it for yourself, it's hard to see how beneficial it can be. Not getting up at the crack of dawn and posting about it, but physically writing things down and then being able to go back and see exactly what you thought in a moment is special. To watch your circumstances change through your own handwriting is something else. When we journal the good and the bad, and it's so often times healing to go back and see that things get hard but they don't last forever. Journaling is the only way to be able to do that. Here are four of my journal entries I copied right into this book and wrote about a week before I graduated. The first is titled:

### First Entry: In Ten Days

In ten days I'll be a college graduate. It's just starting to hit me that life is about to change drastically. All I've known my entire life is school. Thinking about the past four years makes me want to cry tears of joy, something I do not do often. This profound gratitude I feel so deep within my soul is like nothing I have ever felt before. God's plan always includes an exciting adventure, and I guess I have to be ready for the next one. To fully realize that life just keeps going, and we continue to get older, is difficult for me to swallow. As a child, even in high school, I could not imagine being ten days away from college graduation. Today was my last sorority chapter meeting that I will ever have; the actual lasts are starting to come and go. I've been sadder than I thought I'd be the past few days, thinking about leaving the place where I truly began to find myself. As I was on my way to this final meeting, I felt the random sense to look for a rainbow even though it wasn't raining. At first I didn't see anything because I was coming around the corner of my apartment building, but when I got to the parking lot I saw it: a beautiful rainbow with all six colors shining vibrantly. Thank you God for the physical sign that you are right here, faithful in every step. I know your promises won't always feel so tangible, but I know the journey you are taking me on is proof enough that you will always be by my side, mercifully waiting for me to open my eyes to the beauty that surrounds me.

## Second Entry : Anticipation

The anticipation is killing me. In a week my parents will arrive in town for the big weekend. Friday is the day. After we're celebrating at the Derby which we are all looking forward to. I know the weekend is going to be amazing, and I'm not expecting it to be too emotional because of all the excitement. Last night one of my roommates and I talked about how we're not looking forward to this last week because it's over, and now all that's left is waiting around to make it official. I told her I think it'll hit me when it's quiet and all of the excitement dies down. She then starts to cry and maybe for the first time realizes that we are all leaving really soon. This entire year, really since I've been in college, I've thought about how I would feel in these final moments. It's weird to feel like I'm already looking back at the memories of what's to come because I'm anticipating it so much.

## Third Entry: Tomorrow

Tomorrow I graduate from the University of Kentucky. Seeing the goal right in front of your eyes—the one you talked about your entire life up until this point—finally coming to fruition is surreal. I couldn't be more thankful for the experiences and monumental growth that happened during the past four years. It's so hard to believe that it came this quickly and left before my eyes. I so clearly remember saying goodbye to my high school friends the summer before we all left for college. That cool summer night in the driveway, not exactly sure how to get into our cars and not know the next time we'd see each other. How was that four years ago?

I am ready for new beginnings though, I have to be. Fresh starts are so much fun but wrapping things up is not. Endings remind us that everything is temporary. I will so deeply miss living with my best friends; these girls I met four years ago but feel like I've known for a lifetime. Friendships like the ones I've made don't come around often, and I can only pray I find people like the ones I have in Kentucky throughout the rest of my life.

### Forth Entry: I Graduated

I did it! To talk about something for so long as an upcoming event, and then to talk about it in past tense is weird. Did that really just happen? The entirety of senior year it felt like time was in double speed. Graduation weekend, though, time slowed down long enough to take it all in. I'm sure you've experienced that feeling. The really big moments, heavenly or horrible, time slows. The details that you don't remember on the regular, you do during times like this. The weight of the moment makes the memories so clear, and this weekend was definitely one of those.

As my family and I drove to Rupp Arena I felt like I was going to vomit. When I have an overload of emotion I tend to feel ill. It was another one of those moments where I asked myself, "Is this really happening?" Sitting down on the floor in the arena, looking up at all of the families so proud of their student waving, cheering, and yelling their name made me smile. Everyone in those seats sacrificed something for their graduate to be on that floor. The clock strikes six o'clock and the ceremony starts. The president and board of the university walk in and it feels like we're in Hogwarts. The lights go out and the entire arena sings the fight song. Blue flashing lights and fireworks go off and I get a text from my friend saying that the fight song made her cry. Now it's time for the president's speech.

He talks about how we have been prepared to build the past four years and how desperately this world needs builders. He told us to find our why and that the happiest people are the ones who have found the value in serving. He told us we crave success because we want to know we matter. That there is no easy time to do something, but it is our time now. He left us with this: to not forget where we have come from. To remember that we can have both roots and wings. Now it's time for us to walk across the stage and get our diplomas. My college was the first one to go, the College of Fine Arts. I walk across the stage and receive my degree, reunite with my family, and celebrate at one of my favorite restaurants. Tomorrow is Derby Day.

### *Lessons Learned from The Track*

Nobody pays much attention to Kentucky unless they are talking about bourbon or the Derby. Kentucky is an under appreciated, beautiful southern state that goes under the radar most of the time. That first weekend in May, everyone suddenly is interested in going to see what Kentucky is about, specifically to Churchill Downs in Louisville. If you are not familiar with the Kentucky Derby, it is "An annual horse race for three-year-old colts. It was first held in 1875, it is the oldest horse race in the US, and it is the first race of horse racing's Triple Crown." It's almost like a national holiday in the state. There's decor and apparel all over the grocery stores and signage all over town. It's been on my families bucket list to go ever since I can remember. We had Derby parties when I was little, and my mom would make horse-shaped cakes. Of course that's all I remember, the cake. I watched the Kentucky Derby before I knew what it was. Fast forward years later, as a graduation present, my family decides this is the year to go and experience it in real life. The excitement starts months before as we plan our outfits, pick out our accessories, and prepare for the fun weekend that then felt so far away. We wake up early and get ready for the big day ahead. I went with a purple and turquoise pallet, which was ironically the colors of the derby as well, something I didn't know until I was there. I was impressed with myself.

We get to Churchill Downs and are overwhelmed with the grandeur of it all. It looks like a big castle randomly placed in the middle of downtown Louisville. Once inside the gates, it felt like we stepped back in time. Everyone is dressed to the nines. Women's hats are four feet tall, and men's suits are every color and pattern imaginable. People are carrying around a paper booklet with the order of the races and horse's information. It reeks of cigars and alcohol and it's not even noon. We bet on all of the races, walked around the paddock, and got mint juleps which are extremely foul tasting. The day goes by fast and now everyone is getting ready for race number twelve: The Derby. The energy is shifting and it's exciting. Minutes pass and it's time. The horses are now on the track and getting ready to get into the gate. Three, two one, and they're off.

Let me back up for a moment now. The colts that run in the derby are the most elite kind of horse out there, multimillion-dollar thoroughbreds. What no one knew was the backstory of horse number twenty, Rich Strike. The day before the race one of the famous horses and jockeys pulled out, and at the last second the owner of Rich Strike enters him in. The season before he didn't do well, yet his owner still believed in what he was capable of. Everyone was against this horse. His odds were extremely low, 80 to 1 which are almost unheard of. It was the second longest odds in Derby history.

The twenty horses bolt out of the gate like their tails have been set on fire. Most of us have our bets on the most watched, most expensive, and the best odds. The horses are quickly coming around the track and turn the corner to finish the last leg of the race, which was where our seats were. The energy is electric. Everyone has had their eyes on the few horses that were in the lead the entire time, up until now. Rich Strike had miraculously made his way up to fifth, fourth, third, and yet no one is paying attention to him. Only seconds before the finish, he suddenly, almost magically passed the two front-runners. The announcer struggled to identify him and say his name in time. He said, almost in a single breath, "Rich Strike is coming up on the inside... Oh my goodness! The longest shot has won the Kentucky Derby!" To be honest, as soon as the race ended, my family and everyone around us was looking around like, 'Wait, who just won?' It was such a shocking moment that even though we technically saw it with our own eyes, we still didn't really see or believe it. I wasn't prepared to learn such a valuable lesson that day, but I hope it is one I never forget. My mom sent me this post she found on Facebook a few days after the race.

"Where there is life, there is hope. Anything is possible. Don't let anyone count you out. Persistence and determination beat the odds. If you want a life lesson in 2 minutes? Watch the 2022 Kentucky Derby Race. Rich Strike did not have the best starting position. He was not the biggest or best horse. He only made it into the race on account of another horse having to scratch. He was a 30,000-dollar horse against multi-million-dollar ones. It is not always about having the best of everything or being the biggest and most favored. It is about the size of heart and dedication to win and excel in everything you do." I did not expect to learn such a thing as this, and at the Derby of all places. It is no coincidence to me that this happened the day after one of the biggest transitions in my life, to teach me a lesson that everyone needs to hear.

# Chapter Six
## Mortality

Our own mortality is hard to grasp, but even harder when you're a healthy young adult. We tend to think we're invincible. The tragic stories you hear about, secretly, you never think it'll happen to you or anyone you care about. At the very least you pray it won't. Typically, when something tragic and unexpected happens, only then do you realize how fragile life is. How much do we take for granted the miracle of life? We don't acknowledge the normalcy of everyday and how much we like it until it's anything but.

Within my four years of college, there were multiple tragic deaths of people that I went to high school with. None were from my grade and I wasn't close to any of them personally. Just a few months after I graduated college, someone unexpectedly passed away—the first from my grade. Not to sound weird, but this was actually something I had thought about before. I wondered who from my class would die young. Because as awful as it sounds, there's always someone. I never thought about who it could possibly be before it happened, but who it ended up being, I never would have guessed.

Most everyone knew them and the family because their roots run deep within the school. Some would probably even say they could be considered the ideal American family, the type you see in movies. When bad things happen to anyone it's sad, unfair, and unexplainable. With a family like this though you don't expect something tragic to happen to them because they, for whatever reason, seem immune. To distantly watch a family that seemingly has it all experience an excruciating disaster feels even more surprising.

One summer morning, as I lay in bed, I got a text from a close friend of mine saying that this person had passed away. I immediately sat up and reread it, thinking I misunderstood because I was still half asleep. I was so confused and none of it made sense. As the day went on, I quickly realized this news was affecting a large amount of people all over the country. You never expect a classmate of yours, especially at twenty-two, to be on national news because of their sudden death. This affected me more than I thought it would. It's the eerily sobering thought that if this happened to them it could happen to anyone.

At the time of this event, I was reading *Between Two Kingdoms* by Suleika Jaouad, which if you have not read, I highly suggest you do. A quote from her book that I had read just a few days prior put words to this that I cannot. "We call those who have lost their spouses 'widows' and children who have lost their parents 'orphans,' but there is no word in the English language to describe a parent who loses a child. Your children are supposed to outlive you by many decades, to confront the burden of mortality only by way of your dying. To witness your child's death is a hell too heavy for the fabric of language. Words simply collapse." When things like this happen it's an unwanted wake up call for everyone, and when someone's life is cut way too short it makes it all the more obvious.

I started to think about legacy; the one this person left and the one I'm creating now. It's such a big word and rarely used unless we're listening to a motivational speaker or talking about people that have died. We talk about the legacy someone left, but

I want to think about it in the present because it matters now. We arrogantly assume we have plenty of time but, as some know way too well, not everyone is blessed with an abundance of it here on earth. The way we spend our time matters. As AW Tozer says, "When you kill time, remember that it has no resurrection." Spend your time well because it's fleeting.

The existential question we all ask is why do bad things happen to good people? The agonizing answer to this is no one knows. You can't explain away tragedy because no one deserves it. Or, as Diane Lagberg says, "The ability to easily explain away suffering is the clearest indication of never having suffered." Trying to make sense of why something happened doesn't make it better. I really wish it did because I am great at it. That being said I love to moralize situations—we all do. We naturally think if someone is having a rough go of it, it must be because they're doing something wrong and vice versa. Sometimes yes that is the case. Actions do have consequences, but most things are not that simple. Life doesn't fit into a formulaic equation. A+B does not equal C in the kingdom of God. We can be doing all of the "right things," whatever that means, and tragedy still follows us. Sometimes bad people succeed for a while, and often great people suffer for a long time.

As backwards as it seems, I believe we are each handed specific and unique sufferings to be able to bless others in ways that only you can though what you have experienced. I couldn't stop thinking about that thought for weeks after this persons passing. No one wants to listen to people that have never struggled, or at least I know I don't. Frankly, this family is in a situation that can go one of two ways. It can tear and pull them apart, and faith in God can easily and quickly diminish. Or they can honor and trust God like never before, and be a light in the darkness for others that maybe didn't even know there was a light to be found. As I get older, it seems like darkness and light always coexist, like synchronicity.

God entrusts us with suffering to increase our dependence on him. Pain positions us to lean onto him like never before, because to know He's good in the great times isn't that hard. What's awe-inspiring is when the unthinkable happens, and you still believe God is kind. That he actually cares. That even though this is your worst nightmare, it's not a mistake. There wasn't a glitch in the system. From before we're born, God knows the number of our days, and when someone's days end, it gives us a unique opportunity to take a hard look at our own life. Are you living the life you want to be known for? Are you living well? Tomorrow isn't guaranteed, and it's destabilizing when life cruelly reminds us of that.

I distinctly remember thinking on the day of my high school graduation, standing outside of the church all together again for the last time, that there are people right in front of me that I'll never see again. In my head, it was always because I wouldn't not because I couldn't. To see some of your high school classmates for the first time again at a vigil when you just graduated college feels wrong in so many ways. Seeing people come together is beautiful none the less. There's power in numbers, insurmountable strength found in gathering. We desperately need others, and when you feel like you have nothing left is when you realize it most. Living in a world where we can virtually do anything without physically being around people is weird. Is life supposed to be this way? Work remotely, order food to your door without even seeing who brought it, getting in an Uber and not speaking one word to your driver, only having online friends. That is considered normal but where has it left us? More lonely, anxious, and depressed than ever before.

True hearts of people typically show when tragedy strikes. We drop whatever it is and go be with them, just be. We are all way too busy, but then you realize how secondary it all is when your people have gone through the unthinkable. God promises he is near to the brokenhearted, and often uses community to do so.

As I previously mentioned, I was not close, really not even friends, with this person or their family, but I did go to school with them for six years in a class of one hundred and twenty people. When your grade has that few people in it, everyone is going to have some sort of impact on you, great or small. I try so hard to figure out why God works the way he does; in my life and in the lives of others. But I can't. I do know He's not done with this story. He's not done with mine or yours, and until he calls you home, know that he has numbered your days best to glorify him in a way no one else can but you. Don't wait until something bad happens for you to realize this.

Until we get to heaven there's great mystery in this life on Earth. To trust the author of my story that I don't know the end of is very frightening at times. True strength is knowing it's scary and relinquishing the fear despite the vast unknown. Because of this person's life I believe people will find and follow Jesus. I wouldn't say that if I didn't believe it, because honestly, I have no reason to say something like that. I didn't know them in that personal of a way. But for some reason I do, I really do believe it.

## *The Morning*

People love the morning or hate it; I love it. There's something about the fresh wind and the ability to restart that's invigorating. Every twenty-four hours we get the opportunity to begin again; we get to leave behind what was before and look forward to what's ahead. The very set up of our day is an example of the grace that God's given us. Daily renewal is a gift. He doesn't stay in the past so neither should we. Live in the fullness of today and all it has to offer, even if it seems tiresome, boring, and monotonous. We have to learn how to do this because a lot of our life is going to feel that way. We can't wait to find the joy within ourselves or to be happy only in the big moments, because our lives are made up of a million small ones. We can't wait for the thing to happen before we consciously allow our life to begin, whatever the thing is for you. Because what if it never comes? What if it never happens? I don't say that to sound like a pessimist, although I've been called that many times, but I'm definitely a realist by default. If whatever you're dreaming for doesn't come to be, are you going to feel like your life was a waste? I certainly hope not.

Acknowledging that everything ends, including yourself, is healthy even though I am terrified of it. Death has always petrified me. As a very young girl, I'm talking maybe ten years old but possibly younger, I would have panic attacks thinking I was legitimately having a stroke. Panic attacks so severe I would look like I just ran a marathon. Panic attacks so bad I would pee myself. Death scares me just like it does everyone at one point or another, and although I have come such a long way regarding this fear, it still very much bothers me. I'm scared to die even though I know where I'm going. I wish I could pretend like I wasn't aging and that I was invincible like a lot of adults do. But I can't. The realist, researcher, and truth-seeker that I am cannot deny that my days are numbered, and the fact that so many people dismiss this confuses me even more.

Kids love to pretend to be super heroes. Coming of age should make one realize that we definitely aren't. No matter how healthy you are or how tough you seem to be, our broken bodies are going to tire out. Everyone would benefit if we accepted this because awareness allows us to make every day worth something. It propels us forward to have meaningful conversations because what if it's the last chance we have? Live each day with a purpose. Don't walk around aimlessly waiting for the next thing to come, and if today seems too hard to do that, find the courage in the morning. Renewed strength is found there.

## *Circle of Life*

I don't want to get to the end of my life and just then begin to reflect on how good it was. I want to habitually reflect on my life, so when the time comes, I'm at peace with myself and the life I've lived. As I just mentioned, my fear of death has been very prevalent for the majority of my life. The logical part of my brain knew I, at fifteen, probably wasn't having a heart attack. When my life was so hectic with schedules, homework, dance, and typical teenage life, the only thing I felt I could control was my anxiety. I knew what it felt like and I knew how to live in that state, and I eventually became much more comfortable in an anxious state than a relaxed one. What was I supposed to think about if it wasn't that I felt like I couldn't breathe? That might sound funny, but it was a genuine problem I had to solve. And you know one of the best things I did that began to alleviate it? Reading. To get out of my own head and into someone else's.

I tend to go toward the extreme sides of scenarios which result from fear, and the one thing that would sometimes appease my anxiety as a child was this "natural protection" and comfort that I felt the label "childhood" gave me. It put a band aid on my anxiety for a moment but didn't fix anything. I obviously know being a minor doesn't protect you from illness or tragedy. As I close the college chapter, which feels like the final door of childhood, I think about death as I often do, because in a way it feels like my childhood is dying. I'm closing doors I thought would be open longer than they were. I care about these foundational moments, emerging into adulthood, because I don't want to be all over the place decades from now. I don't want to wait years to realize things that I am capable of realizing now. Some people may think your twenties are a time to let loose and be carefree but I don't think they are. Your twenties are foundational. They, more often than not, set you on the path you're going to be on for the rest of your life.

As babies we completely depend on caregivers to do the most basic of needs for us, and as kids we aren't afraid to ask for help and lots of it. It's odd that when we grow into adults the narrative shifts to let's see how much can we do without any help. Why? What's so bad about help and why are we so afraid to ask for it? That is makes us seem weak? Guess what! We are. We can't do this life well on our own. To be the best versions of our self we need other people's help. It's way too difficult to do alone and half the fun. I admire the people that recognize they can't do everything they want to unless others carry some of the burden too. Only for the middle part of life can you possibly pretend like you don't need other people.

*Tuesdays with Morrie* is an incredible piece of art and should be a must read for everyone. It puts life into perspective in such a unique way that has struck a chord with millions of people around the world. One quote that particularly stuck out to me was this, "We all know how to be a child. It's inside all of us. For me, it's just remembering how to enjoy it. Aging is not just decay, you know. It's growth." Enjoy each opportunity to grow and look at aging as a gift because not everyone gets the opportunity. Aging should not be a point of embarrassment or fear but one of accomplishment and peace. You're still here, still going. One foot in front of the other. That is no small feat.

# Chapter Seven
# Hopeful

## *Hope Calls Out Courage*

One of my roommates, senior year, whenever we got into a chaotic situation or something didn't go as planned (which happened often), would say, "Perseverance builds character." We'd roll our eyes and laugh because it's annoying when someone says that in the middle of a problem. I've heard that phrase so many times, but only now seem to realize how much truth is in those three words. Pressing on despite hardships, big or small, builds character that can't be obtained any other way.

That's one of the better parts about growing older: as time goes on, you have more and more evidence that you can get through hard things because you already have. Disappointment is inevitable, but I don't want the small everyday annoyances of life to rattle me, because if I allow that I will be upset every single day. The small annoyances to the worst tragedies we face are redeemed by Jesus. We did not and could never do anything to deserve it, but because of it, we get to have a hope that calls out courage that I most definitely wouldn't have otherwise. I can have hope when life doesn't make sense and courage to stand back up again because God leaves nothing undone. All of the wrong with be made right one day. He keeps every single one of your tears in a bottle to remember and make right what you might feel is lost right now.

## *Victim mentality*

When bad things happen there are two ways to respond: hopeful or hopeless—to believe that the trials you face will be leveraged for good or not. I don't want to be the kind of person that let my circumstances determine my outlook. Because of that, I've never really understood victim mentality. Don't get me wrong; there are plenty of days, and I know there will be more, when I meltdown about whatever less than ideal situation I'm in at the time. It's necessary to feel and move through those emotions because they matter, but it's just as important to not become inundated by them. Bad things happen and we're by products of a fallen world. Things fall apart all the time.

Maybe someone comes to mind that seemingly hasn't had any big tragedies, or "big t" traumas, someone that you believe has led somewhat of an idyllic life. Don't believe that lie you're telling yourself. Whoever comes to your mind absolutely does not, and if they haven't experienced something crushing yet, they will. Surely no one they can get through this life unscathed. Feeling bad for yourself only hurts you, so don't be a victim to your own life.

As I continually and impatiently wait for whatever God has for me in this next phase, it's hard to not feel powerless and useless. I'm trying to lean into the mystery and savor it, as opposed to frantically trying to solve it as soon as possible. If all I do is look forward to the arrival, the reward, the pay check, the party, or the summer vacation, most of my life is going to feel dull, and I know I don't want that.

Any human born into any generation has had a difficult time with waiting. It has never been easy, but there is an added layer to it that did not exist even twenty years ago. Because social media has made life seem like rainbows and butterflies for the most part, and that the things we work for happen as quickly as you can post about it, our culture but especially my generation, deeply struggles because we subconsciously expect instant gratification in almost every area of our life. Real progress takes persistence, which by definition is defined as a prolonged period of time, but we live in a world where we think we can have anything and anybody almost instantaneously. Time and time again throughout history, we've seen successful people choose to delay gratification for the possibility of something so much greater down the road. But now, it seems like as the media gets bigger, these types of stories get smaller, because we don't even have the attention span to listen to the story of how they got there in the first place.

Things change all of the time, for the good and the bad. To be able to hold on to a dream even when the present looks like it'll never happen is so tenacious, something most people aren't willing to do. Something most people can't do, or at the least cannot do well. Uncertainty is extremely difficult to deal with, and to be able to sustain that feeling of limbo because you're driven by a vision, is so admirable. Dreams shouldn't have a time limit, I keep telling myself that, because if they did that would defeat the entire meaning of a what a dream is in the first place. Everything can change in an instant.

## *Desire Leads Direction*

Desire can get a bad rap because wanting can seem selfish. Followers of Jesus are called to be content, generous, and to put others before yourself. To love and serve is the greatest call, so what is an appropriate amount of desire and what isn't? This is what's impossible about big questions like this: no one knows the answer because it isn't one size fits all. There never is, I love and hate that. The freedom to be anything you want to be is exciting, but when trying to figure out how to adult well and prevent heartache and trouble, it feels scary making decisions no matter what direction you choose. One person might tell you you're making the best decision of your life, and the next will say it'll be a big mistake. It's too easy to let other people's opinions cloud what you know deep down is best for you.

People, especially in faith-based communities, don't talk about this enough. What does Godly ambition look like? Or is that an oxymoron. Desire is a good thing, it was designed by God so that we would long for him. If we didn't have it we would get nowhere in life. Desire makes us get up in the morning. I want coffee, so I'll get up. There would be no motivation to do anything if not.

Just as we are all different, so are our desires. They're unique and personal, which makes comparison ineffective and pointless. Why do we do it so often though? Whoever you are comparing yourself with is on a completely different journey than you, and that is good. Our humanness makes us want to compete with one another; it's innate. To celebrate people takes an example and practice, and all comparison does is slow you down and deteriorate your mental health. The more beneficial but harder option is to be grateful for exactly where you're at, because it's getting you to where you're going. Ask God to direct your steps and trust that what happens after is aligned with his ultimate plan.

## *Believing He Can, Trusting He Will*

A misconception with being a follower of Christ is that once you become one life suddenly gets better and easier. That's completely inaccurate, and in some ways, it makes life harder. If you don't believe in God and things don't go the way you would've hoped, it's acceptable to account it to bad luck or something along those lines. As a believer, when something doesn't work out, someone dies, or a relationship fails, this leaves the door open to doubt God and yourself on a deep level if you believe someone higher has a hand in what's happening. I think that's a reason it's so difficult to put all of our trust in God, because we doubt if He truly has our best in mind. I don't want to feel like God is disappointing me. I can handle people or things disappointing me because that's a given. But God? That level of hurt I don't necessarily want to expose myself to fully; that's why faith can feel so daunting. Putting all of your chips in one basket and believing that God's going to use them in the best way possible feels incredibly risky, especially by the world's standards. I tout myself on being logical and for that reason, faith does not always seem sensible to me, but isn't that the essence of it?

It's not that I don't think he can do the things I ask for. I absolutely know he can. What's hard is trusting that he will, and if he doesn't, it's for my own good. Any kind of deep and healthy relationship isn't about getting the other person to do what you want. A relationship with God is not about demanding him to do something, but asking him to meet me right where I'm at and make his presence known in my midst.

In a roundabout way I believe adversity creates clarity because it shows you what and who you care about. Without adversity, we may never learn how to trust and surrender fully. And that is what life is about—surrender. As John Mark Comer brilliantly teaches, becoming more likes Jesus is about doing less not more, but we live in a time where leveling up in every area of your life is of the upmost importance. Trying to better yourself is never going to be a bad thing, but I think too many times it ends up feeling like were chasing after wind. How well is this method really working? Tons of brilliant people will try and sell you on their way to achieve this, but I'd rather receive life from the one who created it, and life advice from trustworthy and wise counsel. Personal values should come from your own convictions, not whatever popular opinion is trending. The still and quiet places are where the most answers are found, and that might be a reason our world is so confused. We live in such an avoidant world that most would rather do anything before having to be alone with our mind, because what might be revealed if we do?

Sitting still for even one minute now a day is impressive. Meditating in the presence of God, even just saying his name, Jesus, changes things. Speaking of prayer, most people have way over complicated it. You can't be good or bad at it, some people just know more church words than you might. Another prayer that's simple and highly effective is the Lord's Prayer, specifically, "Your will be done." It all comes back to that for me. Do I share my requests with God and tell him the desires of my heart? Absolutely, but it's in the same breath of your will be done. I don't want anything outside of that.

With God, all things are possible. I'm sure anyone that grew up in church has heard that a thousand times over. And it's hard to believe. Just because it's hard doesn't mean it's not true. I expect God to show me the best path for my life because he promises he will. He said he will light my path, and I expect him to show up in the tiny details of my life. Put expectations on the promises of God because not only can handle it, he wants to. Cling to the hope of possibility because you can. This allows us to move forward and try again and again and again. It's farther than most people can say they went.

### *Don't Settle*

I never want to miss out on an opportunity because I was too scared to try, because I did that for too long and don't want to live that way again. No one is called to live a comfortable life, but especially as Americans, we completely idolize comfort and seek it at all times. I don't want comfortability to be the goal. Ever. This is nuanced because the reality of what that looks like is different for everyone, and judging others about what they choose to do is to miss the point entirely. I don't want to inadvertently put God in a box because I'd rather have what I deem as comfortable rather than his best; which probably won't be. I'll continue to dream big even when my efforts aren't enough, because impossible is where he begins. The barriers of our effort is a place where God loves to start. All I have to do is take the next step, say the next yes.

That being said I'm afraid many of us let friends and family settle because what we consider loving is actually enabling them to settle for less than what's possible. It's probably not inherently bad, whatever they're doing, but you know they could do so much more. I believe genuine care sometimes looks like sitting down with that person and respectfully asking them, "What the hell are you doing?" I don't want the bare minimum in life. God has given us the opportunity to live life to the full and that's the kind of life I am after.

To step out beyond your comfort zone takes a lot of tenacity and clearly much easier said than done. Our doubtful selves think, "Why would I try to become an actress, doctor, lawyer, makeup artist, or photographer because there are already so many amazing ones out there?" We wrongly assume the world doesn't need our talents because so many others have the same ones. When we do decide to step out in courage, I believe God blesses us with assurance and peace in whatever direction you're headed.

### *Realistic Worldview*

Adults are sublimely taught to look at the world realistically. What does that even mean, realistic. Dreams sadly tend to shrink because as you get older time feels like it's slipping through your hands. And the people that stay dreaming? We assume it's only a matter of time before their heads get shoved out of the clouds. When you come from a healthy and stable place, people don't expect you to go off the grid too much; if it ain't broke, don't fix it type of mentality.

I would assume most are inadvertently taught to play it safe and do the most typical thing: go to college, work, get married, have kids, then watch your kids do the same thing. If we're supposed to model our life after Jesus playing it safe wouldn't be the answer. Jesus constantly did what others wouldn't dream of doing. He touched the sickest people others wouldn't dare go near, had meals with cheaters, liars, and sinners. He willingly bled out for a humanity that was destined for and deserved eternal death. Jesus was anything but predictable, and he did not do things that made sense. If the king of the world was born in a barn, what makes me think I deserve anything more than that? What you have you don't deserve. Everything we have is ultimately His, so why do we grip so tightly to temporary things?

Yes, playing it safe is hard to measure because everyone defines it by different standards; what's risky to some isn't to others. Although anxiety sucks, I've learned maybe earlier than some how to walk through my fears and be brave. That doesn't mean I don't feel afraid, it just doesn't determine what I do. I've learned that the only way out is through, and I know for a fact I wouldn't be as bold as I am today if I first didn't experience debilitating anxiety. I've proven to myself time and time again I can do hard things even when I feel I can't. Anxiety loves to disguise itself as sensible, but because of my years in therapy, I cannot be fooled any longer. I try so hard to never make any decision based out of fear, which was hard not to do just the other day.

On my twenty-third birthday, I flew to see my sister and friend in Dallas, and as I was getting on the plane, the tornado sirens were going off right outside of the airport as a massive storm was approaching. (Tennessee things.) I really did not want to get on this flight, even though the pilot knew if we could board on time, we would be flying away from the storm and miss it entirely. I then started repeatedly texting my parents to accept and allow me to change my flight to the morning. Although I'm adult and can make my own decisions, I wanted my parents to say not getting on this flight was a good idea. I wanted them to validate my fear, which they did not do.

My mom texted back and said, "If this is a decision based out of fear you have to get on the plane."

My dad said, "You know what to do."

I was so incredibly annoyed and replied, "If I die on this flight, I'm coming back to haunt you." Literally choking back tears, I put one step in front of the other, and bravely got on the plane even when it was the last thing I wanted to do. I really didn't want to die on my twenty-third birthday. This example and countless others have taught me I can do hard things right in the middle of my fear.

Young adulthood comes with obvious worries. That is no surprise to anyone. When I spiral into the millions of what ifs, I remind myself I was brave then, and I will be now too. My second-grade teacher was the first person to look me in the eyes and say, "In my classroom we do not play the what if game." We idolize comfort but to truly live, at some point or another, we have to step away from it.

As I chase my dreams, I feel a sense of peace I don't think I would have if I took the easier route. If I wanted to play it safe, I would not move to New York City knowing no one, and live out whatever God has called me to there. Rarely are things handed to us; we usually have to ask and work for the blessing before we get it. We are all created to be world-changers, and I wonder what the world would look like, how it would operate, if we all believed in and tapped into that.

I'm sure by now you can tell I don't sugar coat things, and because of that, the glass half full mentality is not where I naturally lean. In almost any given scenario there's the glass half empty view or glass half full. As a kid, even before I knew what the worst-case scenario could be, I tried to imagine it. It's much easier to make up stories than to acknowledge and believe the truth. For whatever reason, I think that if I can come up with the worst possible situation in my head, and somewhat prepare myself for what that could look like, if or when it actually happens, it won't be as bad as I have imagined it to be. If I thought of it first, I'm somehow in control, which is where most fear grows from.

I've told my therapist plenty of times horrifically graphic scenarios that randomly pop in my head and how they greatly disturb me. She always says, "That'd be awful but you'd get through it." I then look at her with a cocked eyebrow and think to myself, you sure about that? One day, I realized I drastically underestimate myself and way overestimate the situation, whether it's real or not. I assume the problem is something I wouldn't be able to handle and that I would crumble if or when it ever happened. The beauty in this is that when we feel we can't go any farther and are beyond ourselves, the strength of God takes over in ways we can't. Because of that truth, I can live in freedom instead of being bound by never ending fear. If the worst-case scenario ever does happen, you and I would get through it because God's the one who holds it all together.

I don't think I need to inform you that the glass half-empty mentality is really easy. I don't berate myself for naturally thinking this way because, in all honesty, so much of the world is horrifying. The condition it's in and seeing it with the glass half empty is not hard to do whatsoever. To look at all of the brokenness and choose to see the beauty in spite of it? That's powerful. We all have natural tendencies and it's helpful to be aware of them so you don't fall into extremes. Glass too full isn't good either; it's easy to spill over into places where it isn't wanted or appropriate. We don't have to seek darkness out; it's just there. Light has to be found, and where there's light there's life. Remembering there's always beauty to be found makes me want to get up and go look for it.

# Chapter Eight
## Life's a Struggle

*"If there is no struggle, there is no progress."*
*Frederick Douglass*

If everyone let their struggle define their potential, no one would accomplish anything or get anywhere. We'd all be stuck in the past, where we were. Insecurity sneakily looms behind every single person, making it one of the few equalizers we have between us all. It's crazy to think that even the most powerful people in the world wonders if they're enough. The struggles we all experience and relate to connect us on a level that success can't even come close to doing.

People say I'm struggling constantly. I know I do. Up until now, I always thought struggles were something we ourselves could get out of. That some struggle was entirely our own fault, and it would dissipate once we figured out the solution. In some situations, this is true. If I'm struggling to get dinner ready before people come over because I started cooking too late, yes, that struggle is entirely my fault. In other ways, blaming certain struggles on yourself wouldn't even make sense. I'm a little embarrassed to say this is the first time I've thought this way.

A trite phrase we've heard a million times, "You never know what's going on behind closed doors," is something we should be more aware of. Learning to give people grace, especially when struggling, is one of the most beneficial things we will ever do.

Accepting that struggle is and always will be part of life is hard, and I find myself constantly trying to fight it. But that hasn't ever really worked long term for me.

## *We Worry About the Wrong Things*

For most of my life I believed worry was beneficial. That it was protecting and preparing me for potential harm. If I'm completely transparent, it was the deepest belief I held for easily over a decade. Over time, I noticed the things I constantly worried about rarely happened, and the things I could've worried about but didn't occasionally did. A skill that's imperative to learn, especially for anyone struggling with anxiety, is how to not be afraid of being afraid. To be able to look it in the face and say I am stronger than you. It took me what felt like forever to understand that anxiety isn't dangerous, even though at times I just knew I was dying. Does this mean I don't feel anxious anymore? Absolutely not. It catches me at my worst when I hyper-focus on the rare occurrence and then convince myself that because it happened to someone, it's going to happen to me too.

Anxiety likes to make you think you're the exception, that you're the one percent, but the truth is there is an incredibly high probability that you are part of the other ninety-nine percent. Yes, planes crash, but think about how many people fly a day. Chances are so slim that the plane you're on is going to come down. There's risk in everything and to truly live, you just have to accept it. I recognize my own work in this and am definitely proud of myself, but I would not be able to say that without my parent's relentless pursuit to better my mental health. Also, I must mention it's clear I am not a therapist, but I've had years of experience with them so I feel comfortable talking about techniques that helped me.

The things we don't worry about sneak up on us; life's funny like that. Generally, as a society, we are plagued with worry, and one of the bad things about it is that it's very contagious. If one person in the room is anxious, I can guarantee another person will soon feel it too. It's common for people that deal with anxiety to be more perceptive to other's emotions, and I'm one of those people. I can tell when someone isn't totally calm, or if an anxious energy is in the room, I feel it immediately.

As a child I was especially aware of this and wrongly thought if someone else was anxious, I needed to be too. I was not an easygoing kid in the slightest. I only felt comfortable around my parents or grandmas and was the kid who hated sleepovers. I experienced true panic attacks for the first time in fourth grade, and was in therapy before I even knew what that word was. I don't say this for anyone to pity me, but to be an example to others that you can get better. No one is destined to be plagued with anxiety. Just because it might be your natural tendency doesn't mean you don't work to change it. I constantly say to people, "Anxiety is not who I am but something I have to deal with." I do not identify with it. In fact I've found it very beneficial to detach myself from it, because if I don't it's too easy to become its slave.

Thankfully when I went to college a lot of the everyday worry naturally dissipated. Maturing paired with a new environment had a lot to do with it. I'll never forget how much work I put in to get to where I am today though. Never undervalue how far you've come. Why is it so easy to underestimate ourselves? I never thought I would be able to carelessly go out to eat with friends without having a panic attack because I was afraid I would have an allergic reaction. I never thought I would live in New York City alone for a summer during college and absolutely thrive. That would've seemed impossible just a couple years ago.

When my anxiety was out of control, I would remind myself of how many times I had been afraid of passing out, not being able to breathe, getting sick, or whatever other health crisis I was afraid of, and ask myself how many times any of that actually happened. If you can't tell, all of my anxiety revolves around health-related issues. Because of my very strong-willed personality, it took years for that to click in. Although anxiety can physically be incredibly uncomfortable, it is not threatening or emergent. It helps me to think of these physical symptoms like bate luring me into a frenzy. I took it so far once that I begged my pediatrician, yes my pediatrician, to let me get an EKG. No kid should even know what an EKG is much less be asking for one. I was totally convinced something was horribly wrong, and I bet you can guess the results. Totally healthy and normal.

As I'm sure you know, things rarely, if ever, work out the way we wish or thought they would, so what good does worry do? Time and time again I hear people say, "this isn't how I would've planned out my life, but it's way better than I could've imagined." Struggle is like that too. I wouldn't want to go back to that place, but I also wouldn't want to change it. That takes the pressure off to not micromanage every aspect it. This is obviously way easier said than done, so much of life is like that. Wouldn't it be great if these sayings were just as easy to live out as they were to say? I really thought anxiety kept me safe but the truth is we're never really one hundred percent safe, no matter how secure we think we are. Getting in the car today is a slight risk, but one most are willingly to take. There are much more dangerous things as opposed to getting in a car, and it's wise to be cautious of them and not abuse free will. But generally we make up what's risky and what isn't, and it's insightful to see what we deem worthy of fear. And then maybe think about why.

I know I don't want to be paralyzed by complacency due to fear, and exposing myself to risk, which really means exposing myself to the world, is an invitation to trust that. It's asking for strength for today and hope for tomorrow. Even if God's plan for your life seems senseless and out of your realm of possibility, it isn't out of God's. Your plans might even make more sense on paper, but the truth is the safest place to be is within God's will for your life. He will not fail you.

## *Growth and Comfort Don't Go Together*

A question I've been contemplating a lot recently is this: Can you grow and be comfortable at the same time? In my experience, no, because growth is typically very uncomfortable. During major growth spurts as a kid, it sometimes physically hurt. Most of us want to know how things pan out, and we want to know that wherever we're headed is some place good. The times I've changed for the better were the most uncomfortable I've ever been in my life. It felt like I was growing new skin, but those growing pains were essential to my formation. We cannot spare ourselves from pain as much as I wish we could. Problems follow us wherever we go, but a lot of the time these problems end up benefitting us and others in the long run.

In the height of my therapy going, it got to the point where my family could tell without me saying that I had been that day because of the way I acted after. It drained me, and occasionally I was more agitated after a session than before I went. As time went on, it wasn't so intense, and the change wasn't so scary. It was exciting to see glimpses of how I could live instead of how I was before. This might sound odd, but letting go of the anxiety I tightly held onto felt like grief in a way because, at that point, I'd been living like that for so long. Anxiety was more comfortable than calmness because it was my normal.

One of the comforting things about change, risk, and growth is that it gets easier overtime. Avoiding difficulties feels better in the moment, but is only making things harder in the future. What feels impossible today might not feel so tomorrow, but we have to do things to get that place. Hoping, wishing, and even praying for a better life isn't going to get you there. Decide to make a change, get up, and go. I tell myself frequently, "If you don't want a typical life, you can't do typical things."

### Don't Over Complicate

In ways the human experience is nuanced and complicated, and in other ways it is overtly simple. We love to make things much more complicated than they need to be. I believe life can be as complicated or as simple as you make it. Sometimes we forget that we chose the path we're on, that the general trajectory you have a say in. If certain things stress and make you unhappy, change something. The answers to our problems are usually much simpler than we'd like to imagine, because it's easier to complain than to do actually do something about it.

My senior year of high school my psychology teacher would famously say, in varying situations, "It ain't that deep." At the time, she was teaching seventeen and eighteen years old how the mind works in the midst of embarking on one of the biggest life changes we were ever going to experience. Students would come to her for advice and the conversation would often end with her saying, "It ain't that deep." Look at the situation right now that's causing you stress, and ask yourself if this is going to matter in one, five, or even ten years. If the answer is no, then the problem isn't worth the attention you're giving it. Some things are that deep and deserve ample attention and care, I'm not diminishing those experiences, but I do think most would be better off if we took a step back to ask ourselves if the thing that's bothering us is really worth losing sleep over.

### *Apologize*

This is one of the biggest things we overcomplicate. It's surprisingly difficult for people to own up to their faults. I've not met anyone who loves to admit when they're wrong. As a kid, when learning how and when to apologize, I remember wanting to crawl out of my skin because I hated it so much. Even if I knew an apology was necessary, the act of saying it out loud made me physically so uncomfortable. You'd hope and somewhat expect kids to grow out of this, but we all know adults who will not, for the life of them, apologize and admit when they messed up. Excuse after excuse is made, and for what? To pretend like you're above making mistakes? Because we know no one is. Why is it so hard for people to admit what they've done? Why can people not face the music they started?   My best guess is it's because when you admit wrong doing, it inadvertently puts you in a vulnerable position. You are saying I missed the mark and have fallen short. We don't like thinking about the fact that we have to capability to deeply hurt others, but we all do. I understand some things are inexcusable and deserve ample consequences, but forgiving others as well as giving them grace is what we're called to. Not begrudgingly say a few words that mean nothing to you and then stay bitter for the rest of your life. That's only hurting yourself. Personally, I'm selfish and don't want my life to be any harder than it needs to be, so if forgiving will do that for me, I'll do it. Two simple truths I will always try my hardest to live by are these: Tell the truth and say sorry. We nod our head and know that's the honest and upright way to live. We learned that in preschool, but some of the simplest lessons are hardest learned.

## *Hard Lessons*

I've had my fair share and here are just a few examples. I have been a confident driver from day one and wasn't afraid of the road when learning to drive. This, in turn, led to a speeding issue. As any parent does, they tell their child again and again to not speed. Of course I nodded and agreed, but whenever I got in the car, I'd seem to forget that. I wish I would've listened to them without having to get in trouble with the law first. Much less four times. Within the first year of having my license I got pulled over not one, two, or three times. Four. The best part? Of those four, two of them happened directly after one another in the same week. I got pulled over on Monday, and twenty-four hours later, on Tuesday, it happened again. I know what you're thinking. I'm an idiot! And in those moments, I absolutely was. The first two times I got a warning, which was very generous, and the third time I did get a ticket but neglected to tell my parents for weeks because of how embarrassed I was. Oh, and the fourth time was for expired tags. What was especially terrible about that time was that the police pulled me over into my school parking lot one morning just as everyone was getting there. I walk into school, and I overhear people saying, "Who was in the white jeep that got pulled over this morning?" It was me. I am so happy to report I have not been pulled over since.

    Lessons learned for whatever reason happen often in the car for me. Just like the speeding rant my parents went on, I was constantly told to bring my purse inside whenever I left my car. Even though I always locked it, they assured me that does not mean someone might bust a window and steal it. In my seventeen-year-old brain, I took this more of a suggestion and never thought it would happen to me. I lived in a very safe area and naively did not think that kind of thing would happen in my town. That's what we all think until it happens.

    One night after dance ended, which was past nine o'clock, my sister and I were going to get into the car, and as I approached it, I saw that the window behind the driver's seat was shattered, and you guessed it, my purse was gone. I was genuinely too shocked to speak and was ridiculously mad at myself for not listening to my parents, and once again having to learn the hard way. As a teenager, especially, it seemed as if the extreme had to happen to me before it finally clicked. Don't be this way; it makes life a lot harder than it needs to be.

    Lesson number three is to never swear anything off because you never know what might happen. I'm at the point where "Never say never" is a frequent phrase I say to people, because my life has proven that to be true. Going into college, I swore I'd never be in a sorority, and was never the girl that wanted to partake in something like that. I believed it was the easier way out of making friends and didn't want help. The stereotypes I believed made me not want to be a part of it even in the slightest. When I got to college, of course all the girls I had become friends with were in a sorority, and weirdly, they were almost all in the same one. My second semester of my freshmen year, I joined said one and stayed all four years. I learned most of the Greek life stereotypes aren't true, or are only true if you want them to be. There is depth wherever you go if you're willing to find it. Don't count yourself out because of what you think you know, I've done that one too many times. The things we regret are most often the things we don't do, as opposed to the things that we do.

This last lesson is about gossip and happened a mere few weeks ago. In case you didn't know, girls talk. A lot. Gossiping is too easy and gets out of control sometimes. So, alas, I tell you this very humbling story. My friend and I were at a dance concert to watch one of our friends perform, and as I flipped through the program I noticed a girl that I didn't know personally, but recognized because she took graduation photos around campus as do I. I pulled up her profile on Instagram to show my friend and said, "Oh look, this girl takes pictures but they aren't that good." What happens next you would hope only happens in movies, but I'm here to tell you they certainly do happen in real life.

One seat over from me, a man pipes up and says, "Oh, that's my daughter, and this is her camera." (As he lifts up said camera to show me.) This girl's father was taking photos for her during the show that she was also dancing in. I didn't say anything. I turned to my friend, utterly speechless, both of our eyes as wide as they'd go, trying to process what just happened. We stared at each other for at least a minute and could not speak. It was funny because if you know me, you know, something like this just makes sense. Weird things tend to happen before I wake up and learn something. This lesson is simple: Do not talk about people; you literally never know who is sitting right beside you.

## *Scarcity Mentality*

If you believe this, you're going to feel like you're regularly struggling. It's a valid fear that many face: Is there enough room for me? We learn this early on in the lunch room or outside on the playground, is there room for one more? Whatever career or industry, thoughts like this can take over quickly, and it can become very worrisome. First and foremost, there is enough room for you and for me. I refuse to believe that there isn't. I have to remind myself of this truth every single day. Knowing that a lot of people want the job I do, have the same exact dreams as me, and are incredibly talented is nerve-wracking. How could it not be? A photographer that has been a mentor and inspiration from the beginning gave me a piece of advice I've never forgotten. She said, "It's so much easier and relaxing to think about wanting one slice of the pie. To eat the whole thing would be unhealthy and way too much for one person. Focus on obtaining that one piece and taking your share. We tend to think that we want all of the success, all of the pie, but we really don't." This not only allows me to feel peace with where I'm at, but allows me to celebrate other people's success, to not constantly feel like I'm in some sort of competition with everybody. It's harder to be jealous when you believe that everyone is welcome, important, valuable, and that their success is not a hinderance to your own.

Most of my friends, correction all of them, got jobs before me, and I would be lying if I said I wasn't at times extremely sad, jealous, and insecure about it. This is the first time in life where it really feels like my worth and talent is measured by what I do or who I'm with. Emphasis on 'feels.' I know my worth is not measured by a job, a salary, or a person, but it sure feels like it. I fight that lie daily. Understanding that what other people have, whether it be a job, a house, a kid, or whatever else, was never meant for me or you. The job they have is not the job for you because if it was, you would have it. What's meant for you won't pass you by. The doors that God opens cannot be shut, and the doors that don't open are not from God. When you believe that, you're going to have peace that does not make sense to most. In today's world true satisfaction is almost impossible to grasp, because so many of us put all of our hope in things that at the very best will give you a sense of momentary happiness or relief. God is the Price of Peace, and I think he is what you're longing for.

# Chapter Nine
## Authentic Self

*<u>Made on Purpose</u>*

It's safe to say we all wish we didn't have certain qualities about ourselves and want certain features that we will never possess. I have from an inward and outward perspective. I'm very petite, 5 feet 2 inches to be exact, and am not built like a stick. I don't love being short and will not give anybody a reason to look down on me, but the reality is most everyone literally has to. My lips and nostrils are noticeable uneven. My eyelids are extremely hooded. One of my eyebrows has a huge dip in it, and it frequently resembles a worm. I struggle with acne. Those are just a few things I notice when staring at my face. I'm unfortunately no stranger to self-hatred and know what it feels like to be so uncomfortable in your own body you feel like there's no other option but to change it.

My sister and I both struggled with severe eating disorders a couple years apart from each other. It's strange because in some ways no one could have seen this coming, but in other ways, it was perfectly set up to happen, let me explain. If you didn't know, anxiety and Obsessive Compulsive Disorder go hand in hand. And no, OCD is not just organization and cleanliness; it's much more complicated than that. My anxiety about my body changing as a teenager led to hyper-focusing on what I ate, what I did, and what I wore, which led to an eating disorder. Growing up as a dancer, I'd love to say that this is uncommon, but the amount of girls I know that have had serious eating issues along with wild amounts of body dysmorphia is incredibly alarming. I do not know one dancer, and believe me I know a lot, that has not at the very least struggled with body dysmorphia and at the worst been sent off to residential treatment multiple times for life threatening eating disorders. Anorexia specifically is a big part of my family's story. I specifically say family because this is something that does not affect just you. It affects everyone around you deeply.

My parents played no role in the development of this for my sister or me, which unfortunately is a large factor for many people. We were taught how to intuitively eat before we knew what that meant. The only rule we had regarding food was, "Eat when you're hungry, and stop when you're full." What people don't realize is when you start to mess with and control the natural rhythms of your body, it's very difficult to get back to a healthy and intuitive place. Growing up, there was always an abundance of food around and nothing was off-limits. Friends always wanted to be at our house because we had the best snacks and food. My parents are in shape, have never really dieted, and live a balanced life with exercise and nutrition. How did both of their daughters end up with anorexia?

On the flip side of that, developing an eating disorder could have been a little bit more predictable. Our doctors and therapists told both of us that we had outside factors that unfortunately made the perfect cocktail for this sick illness. We both are severely allergic to nuts and because of that, learned how to read nutrition labels much earlier than any kid should. This, of course, couldn't be helped. For our own safety, we had to learn how to do this at a much younger age than most people. Some adults don't pay attention to food labels, and we both had to know how to do that by the time we could read. We had no choice.

Secondly, and I believe most prominently, was the fact that we were a part of the dance community in an affluent area. We danced at competitive studios all throughout middle and high school and for our school's dance team. Speaking of, not only was the dance program elite, so was everything else. The academics, the athletics, everything was above average, and almost half of my grade signed to play college sports. That isn't normal. I'm thankful for the educational experience I had, but I'd be lying if the very elitist atmosphere didn't play a role in the spiral that a lot of kids face, myself included.

Do not hear what I'm not saying. In no way am I bashing my school. High school is a very difficult time for most kids anywhere, and I don't believe my small private school played a special role in the specific struggles I and others faced. The standard of success that was put on the students though created a lot of unnecessary pressure. The undertones our teachers and coaches implied, whether conscious or not, was if you didn't win, we're not even going to talk about the fact that you came in second or whatever place or score you got. Some people excelled and thrived in this environment, others not so much.

School was always harder for me than for my sister; she's naturally very book-smart. The first time I felt less than in a classroom was in the first grade and I remember it clear as day. I was asked to say the vowels aloud and didn't know them. From that moment, really since I've been in school, I've never felt smart. I never failed any classes, and I almost always made A's and B's, in all subjects except math, which was frequently a C. I had a tutor from sixth all the way to twelfth grade, which I felt at the time was incredibly embarrassing. I couldn't do my math homework by myself which, in my head, obviously meant I was stupid.

As an incoming sixth-grader at the private school, that I attended sixth through twelfth grade, we were required to set a goal for our grade point average and at the end of each semester. If we didn't meet it, we had to stand up in front of our entire class, letting everyone know. How ridiculous and mortifying is that? I recently went through my sixth-grade binder that my mom saved and at the top of one of my papers I wrote, "I have fallen off. I didn't succeed." I was eleven. I can guarantee you I did not come up with that phrase on my own. I heard it, then emulated it. We were taught that if we turned something in on time, it was late, that we lazy and slacking off if we weren't the first person to turn something in. The competitive nature of this school was one of the first things you learned. Shaming people into doing the right thing seemed to be the tactic, and at times felt like the message often was conformity instead of curiosity. Was it? Probably not. Is that the language that I have found years later to explain that experience? Yes. The problem with this is that when perfect seems to be the standard, it undermines anything great. That is not a great thing to learn as a kid, because it's inadvertently setting you up to where very little measure up. And I would hate to be that kind of person.

A lot of people were above the mean in one area or another, whether that be academically or athletically all throughout school. The bar was so high, that even if you were doing well, it sometimes didn't seem like enough. Without me realizing this, it got into my psyche. There was a very real, albeit somewhat disproportionate amount of emphasis on honors and AP classes, which obviously I was never recommended for. This is not a bad thing at all and some people absolutely do need that extra push.

What was a very real problem, though, was the distinction between the normal level classes and the upper-level ones. We got called "The regs kids." To me it felt like you were either in the regular classes because you didn't try as hard as your peers, or you were just dumber than they were. When you aren't either of those things, it's difficult to be called a "regs kid," and that's what I was considered for seven years. It got to the point that during my freshmen year I fully convinced myself I had a learning disability. I insisted that my parents take me to get tested because surely this test would show what I was lacking. To no one's surprise but mine, I tested completely normal in all areas. I never personally experienced bullying from anyone about being in these classes, but I often times heard jokes about being "regular," and it was not funny to me.

My sister can attest to this. She was in the honors classes and was awarded for having the highest grade in French multiple times. She saw my struggles with school and how it made me feel, and then went to her honors classes and saw how some looked down, intentionally or not, on people in the normal "standard" ones. When adults put so much emphasis on honors and AP's, impressionable high schoolers perceive that as how they are deemed valuable. I wish kids could learn sooner that worth doesn't come from obtaining an A in an honors class or receiving a piece of paper that says you're on the headmasters list. Life is so much bigger but as a high schooler you can't see or understand that. That is when trustworthy adults should step in and help you see this truth, but they didn't. They egged it on more.

It's very paradoxical the reality that a lot of kids face, not just at the school I went to but in the surrounding areas as well. The county I grew up in is the wealthiest one in the state of

Tennessee, and it's up there with some of the wealthiest in the country. Not only did we all have what we needed, most of us had everything we wanted too. On paper, we were living the dream, no issues. Don't get me wrong, some kids—no matter where you grow up—are high school heroes. Thank God I wasn't one of them.

Something I didn't expect when I graduated high school was the amount of people that would transfer back home to the small bubble of safety that they've always known. It wasn't that they were not prepared to move away and go to college. We were all set up for success and had an infinite amount of resources to thrive. For some, pushing beyond the comfort of the suburb was not as easy as they had originally imagined. This is not a dig to those people whatsoever although it could sound like it. There's absolutely nothing wrong with moving back home and sticking to your roots. I also believe it's very easy to fall back into old ways of life as an adult, especially if you stay in the same place that you "thrived" in as a teenager. How much can you really thrive as a teen though. Subconsciously, I wonder if some fall into old patterns because they're afraid to try anything new. When you believe God has your best interest at heart, it's easier to live a daring life because you know He's got you wherever you go.

Mental health is a buzzword and it's great that we live in a society that now acknowledges it. But I can't help but notice the increasing amount of kids in therapy along with taking antidepressants. At the very least it's noticeable, and at the worst it's extremely distressing. Not because any of that is bad or wrong; I participate in both and have for years. I'm the first person to advocate for therapy and medication. I have clear memories of talking with classmates at the lunch table, sometimes with people I wasn't even that close to, and the conversation would revolve around what antidepressant we were taking. Most of us there had the best of the best; I can't speak for everyone, but most. Why then did so many struggle with mental health issues at such a young age?

I do not know other people's situation, but speaking for myself, I was in therapy for years before I finally agreed to take medicine. The harsh truth is I was not making the progress that needed to be made, and the most effective way to treat true mental health disorders are therapy and medication combined. It's an interesting place we're in though with antidepressants, because they're prescribed with very little concern. With the abundant amount of talk and experience surrounding mental health on the internet, young people especially think they have severe mental health disorders when they might not. And not everyone needs medication to fix the normal and depressing parts of life, but that was not the case for me. My pediatrician told my parents when I was a newborn that she could tell I had an anxious disposition. Even in the womb my mom recalls that I was extremely still, but when she was in a loud environment I would jump. I worked endlessly in therapy for years before finally surrendering to medication. I do not take these topics lightly.

Back to the high school antidepressant lunch table talk, there is one obvious answer and others that aren't so clear as to why the people I grew up around flippantly talked about therapy and medication. Children at a private school go to therapy because they can afford it. I'm not blind to the fact that therapy is a privilege not everyone is lucky enough to participate in. You would hope that if certain children have everything they need and want, they wouldn't struggle to the degree at which a lot do.

I just got very sidetracked. We were talking about eating disorders and dance. In that small world of dancers the pressure to look a certain way is very real and everyone knows it but no one likes to talk about it. We're in sports bras and booty shorts staring at ourselves in the mirror for hours on end multiple days a week. Adults are staring at our bodies and correcting its placement. We're taught how to be highly aware of our body—the way it moves, looks, and acts, but at the same time taught how to ignore it. Pain? Push through. Exhaustion? Hardly worth mentioning because everyone is. There is an underlying narrative that we can falsely manipulate our bodies to look a certain way because we can do things with them that a lot of people can't. This is why I think eating disorders and aesthetic based sports are like birds of a feather.

The stereotypical body type for a dancer is thin with muscle, but not too much, of course; you would never want to look bulky. If you don't have abs and can't see your ribs when you breathe, you might want to lose a few pounds and maybe even download MyFitnessPal to keep yourself in check. When my peers and I started to fill out and not look like twigs any more, major concern arose. The prepubescent body type is what is desired, so when my body began to change, I felt wildly out of control. It's also alarming when your teacher says she wishes her body looked like a twelve-year old. When we as a team would stand in front of the mirror, with our thirty-five-year-old coach nonetheless, and lean forward to see who could stick their collarbone out the most. Plus the underlying tones that if you were anything over a size four, you were big. Or when girls were clearly a size small or medium but our teacher gave them a size large because that's how she saw her. Before I would eat a chocolate bar with maybe four ingredients for a snack, and now I could not begin to fathom doing that. The one hundred calorie snack packs filled with a laundry list of preservatives was no problem though. My diet and exercise hadn't changed but my body was. What was happening to me?

These thoughts utterly consumed me and ramped up my anxiety, which led me to feel like I had to control something, anything. Assignments flowing left and right, dance practice almost every day, and typical teenage insecurities felt like too much. As a fourteen-year-old, controlling the calories I put into my body and the number I saw on the scale felt like the only thing I could achieve when the rest of my world felt totally out of my hands.

The realization that took me too long to get to was that no one cares what I look like. The only one thinking about my body is me, and if other people genuinely do care about the way I look, they have a problem that me loosing five extra pounds won't fix. Most people have the wrong perception of what an insecure person is. We think it's someone who doesn't care about themselves at all and refuses to attribute anything to themselves. That is probably true in some scenarios, but I think the most insecure people are the ones that think about their body too much and flaunt it. The people who maybe even use other peoples' bodies to make them feel better about their own.

An eating disorder is an extreme form of compulsive patterns, so someone with these disordered ways most likely feel like they can't stop thinking about, or acting upon whatever their specific habits are. These patterns that were so easily created become ridiculously hard to break. I never meant to have an eating disorder, most people don't. I didn't know what I was doing until I no longer recognized myself. I started to believe that if I ate one cookie my body would inflate like a balloon and change immediately. After eating anything I deemed bad, I would constantly look at myself in the mirror, or take photos of my body to compare what they looked like just a few hours ago. I weighed upwards of five times a day and when my nutritional therapist, who worked wonders but scared the living hell out of me, told my parents to immediately take the scale out of the house, I cried hysterically on the couch for two days. And I am not a crier. If I cry, I am extremely upset. Once the scale was out of the house, I would lie about where I was going and would drive to my grandparents' house just to weigh myself. Most teenagers lie about where they're going to hang out with people or do things they shouldn't. I lied about where I was going to weigh in. The first time I met this nutritional therapist, she pulled up her chair right beside me, looked me dead in the eyes while handing me paper and a pen, and said I should start planning my funeral if I was going to continue living this way. She meant business.

    I felt like I couldn't stop thinking about myself and that anorexia controlled me. It was a beast I seemingly brought on, and now it was way bigger than I ever intended to be. What is magnificent about our complex brains is that they are more powerful than we could ever comprehend. They can make us believe that our thoughts control us rather than us controlling them. Thankfully that isn't true. If you want to change, you can. You have to want it though, other people can't make you.

    No matter who you are, there are going to be physical attributes we wish we could change. On my bad days, there are things about my personality I wish I could change too. Sometimes I wish I was an extravert, and for the longest time I thought the fact that I didn't love to be around a lot of people for an extended amount of time was weird. That I wasn't any fun because of that. I'm very blunt, opinionated, and my tendency is to see the world in black and white. I have very tough skin and have to remind myself that a lot of other people are not that way, so I usually have to be much gentler than what is natural for me. If you were to ask my friends and family what comes to mind when thinking about me, most of them would say bold within the top three answers. I love that about myself, and for the most part I'm unafraid to be me. I've always understood that not everyone will like you, and to even try to pursue such is impossible. Of course there have been times when I've questioned why I was made the way I am. We all do it, and it's not a bad thing to wonder. I believe the way I was made will, in time, push me into the best version of myself. As a young adult, we can only begin to see glimpses of our story and how all of these moments will coincide one day.

As I made brand new friends again for the first time in college, I realized one of the attributes I found most attractive was confidence. That is what drives people to listen to others. We don't care about others because of the number on the scale, incredible clothes, a flawless face, or money. Well, we shouldn't. If I was supposed to be a sensitive five-foot-ten extrovert, I would be. We have gotten it so wrong in thinking that healthy looks a certain way.

For me to pretend like I am an extremely bubbly and outgoing person is just never going to be the case; that's not who I am. Too many of us spend so much time trying to be like someone else. We say, "If only I looked like her or acted like him, I would be happy and successful." No, you wouldn't. We idealize other people's outward lives and measure it with the worst moments of our inward ones. The specific things you bring to the table can only be brought by you. Start believing in the miracle that you are. You aren't your net worth, your occupation, or your relationship. You're not complete, whole, because "You're somebodies somebody." You're enough because you're you. Every part of you is here for a reason, and what you believe about yourself matters.

## *Authenticity Over Approval*

I've never been considered a people pleaser but know plenty who are. To a degree I care, because if I truly didn't at all that would be concerning. In no way am I a pushover and am hardly ever persuaded to do something I don't want to do. In college especially my desire to want to be different only intensified. Even something as trivial as clothes I never wanted to be wearing what other people were. I didn't want people to think of me as a "typical college girl," which is hilarious because in a lot of ways I was one. There is nothing wrong with being that way and loving it, but I just never thought any of that was worth my time. Worrying about a dress to wear at formal and where the pregame was? I could not even for a few minutes pretend to care. This was fine to an extent, but it's been somewhat hard to relate to people my age because what many consider to be fun, I consider dull and at times wildly stupid. It amazes me that people truly have the mentality that "It isn't a problem until you're out of college," or some really can't see that they're only having fun if alcohol is involved. Your twenties, your life really, doesn't have to be filled with drunken nights and hungover mornings. It can be adventurous and playful without the extra help that make things "fun." We're too worried about being perceived as cool by others, we can't even begin to discover what we actually like and care about. Social media has not helped this at all. Strive to be authentic, rather than lapping up scraps of approval from people that probably don't care. I fear it's going to take people my age twice as long to find out who they really are because so much of their life is clouded by what's trending on TikTok. Subliminal messaging that approval from others is of the upmost importance is so embedded into everything we consume. I refuse to be defined by people's perceptions of what is deemed cool or weird.

## *Obsession with Youth*

As a culture we are absurdly obsessed with youth. I admittedly fall into this category like millions of others because it's popular and "normal" to think this way. Normal doesn't always mean right or good though. Twenty-year-old get Botox now, preventative treatment it's called. Think of all the billions of dollars invested into skin care products that promise the reduction of fine lines and wrinkles. A fast metabolism and having skin that doesn't fold or move are just a few things that characterize youthfulness. We glamorize the physicality of youth but foolishly neglect the lackluster parts about it like insecurity, awkwardness, and doubt. I think this is one of the many reasons young people are confused about this age. We know what young adulthood feels like because we're in it, but most older adults glamorize it. Are we talking about the same time period? Do older adults not remember this time in their lives, this in between phase where young adults are trying to find their rhythms in the world? It is much harder than people told me it would be, and I wonder if it's because they forgot. After all, memories often times are how we perceive a situation. They're what we think happened not exactly what happened. We all idealize the past, and the present for that matter, so I'd say most look back and remember the highlights. Maybe they look back with rose colored glasses but forgot that just because you're young and free doesn't mean you don't struggle. It appears in all stages. It's funny because when you are young it seems like you should have this natural confidence in how you look, and when you get a little older confidence in what you do. That is not the case. Confidence doesn't spontaneously appear at a certain age or a certain position and it is not something you can buy.

When I was in the thick of my anorexia I frequently said, "If I just lost one more pound, I would be satisfied with how I looked." Then I would be confident. That was the smallest I have ever been, and ever will be, yet the most insecure I've ever felt in my life. And you know what's even worse than that? I've never received more compliments and praise about my body than when I was the sickest. One of the biggest hinderances in recovery is other people. They absolutely fed into the lies I was telling myself. That I was prettier, more attractive, healthier, because you could see my eight pack—I was ripped.

They didn't know I lost my period for over a year, my hair was falling out, and my acne was ten times worse than before. No one saw the torment that was going on inside of my body and I eventually learned no number on the scale would have satisfied me. Losing one more pound or getting just a few more units of Botox will not make you more confident. We think these physical things will help aid in our outer and surface level issues, but they never will because this is a soul problem. True beauty is not found in a mirror, and deep down we all know it. No one's gravestone is going to say, "Had a great body." When has anyone ever gone to a funeral and talked about how great they once looked? We don't talk about it then because, in the end, it doesn't matter. So why does it matter now? Your physical body is truly the least interesting thing about you.

Extremely impressionable children, and adults too, look up to celebrities and influencers who have had work done and wrongly assume they were dealt bad genes because they don't have big lips, perfect teeth, and high cheek bones. People that are thirty think they're old because the ideal look now is someone who is eighteen, and eighteen-year-olds now certainly don't look like how most of us looked at that time.

Taking care of yourself and wanting to be healthy is important, but many of us make it the ultimate thing. Taking care of yourself, to me, is more about how you treat your body in the process, and maybe even consider why you're doing whatever you're doing in the first place. The majority of us do not do this. We'd rather just do and deny ourselves the reality of a situation. The thing about that though is when you deny what's really going on it will come back later. You're exactly the way you were created to be as cliche and annoying as that sounds. You'll save a lot of money too. As I've gotten a little bit older, I weirdly like to see physical reminders of my humanity. The bumps, discoloration, unevenness and bruises on myself remind me I can never be perfect. And that is something I need to be reminded of frequently.

You might not think this problem is as big as it is but it goes deeper than you'd assume. As you know I am a researcher by nature, and one day I came across a study about different factors that can cause anorexia and other types of eating disorders. One of the components that particularly stood out to me was how subconsciously some struggle in this way to keep their body in a childlike state, to halt the maturation process without even realizing it. Essentially, being so uncomfortable with development, some unconsciously try to stop the physicality of it. This blew my mind because I had never heard anyone talk about this before. But if I look back to when I struggled with my eating disorder, and when most start, it was right in the midst of when my body was changing the most. When my body changed from looking like a girl's and started to look like a woman's.

### *All Are Valuable*

The emphasis on youth right now in some manner is amazing and in others not so much. As a society, we now realize that younger generations can offer deep insight and great value to the world at the age they're at, instead of waiting until they're "old enough" to do so. Of course, I haven't been around to see multiple generations come and go. I don't think it's always been this way. Elders in the past were of the upmost importance and what they said went. No one questioned the system and everyone looked to them for what to do and how to act. Not that my generation doesn't do that, but the focus back then was much more on adults and elders as opposed to the young. That has definitely reversed, especially in America.

We treat young people like they have the ideal stance and way of life, almost like we're more evolved than they are. As bad as it sounds, it feels like it's out with the old, in with the new mentality. To an extent, especially as a woman, this is great because for too long, we didn't have any say or value unless it was mothering children at home, and the kids at home most definitely didn't have any sort of right to even suggest how something could be. We need to get to the place where we value all voices. We think and say we want equality and justice for all, but that isn't the way most people act. For the most part, we all love and accept people that look different than us, but when it comes to the people that think different than us? We can't seem to handle that very well. When did we become so easily offended? So much so, that we in turn, have cut ourselves off from whoever thinks differently. People who disagree with you shouldn't threaten your value system, because if you really believe what you say, it wouldn't. Who cares? We all have the freedom to believe what we want to. Or is it just about being right? We treat people as if they're going to break if we tell them we don't agree with them. If you don't see that as a problem, you should.

So again, I ask: why do young adults fear growing older? One, we obsess over everything related to the young and in turn disregard the old even if we don't realize it. Why would we ask an eighty-year-old about life advice and wisdom when you can ask Google, listen to a podcast (on 1.25 speed at least), or YouTube it. An old person's life is slow, and most of us genuinely cannot sit still for five minutes without being entertained in one way or another. We think we can't learn anything from them because all they do is sit around quietly, but that in and of itself is something we all desperately need to learn how to do.

You never hear people say I wish I was eighty, but if someone says I wish I were twenty, we don't think twice. The cool thing about being eighty, I assume, would be the retrospect. That is one of the beautiful things about growing older, leaning back and trusting because you've had decades worth of proof that things work out. My short life thus far has proven that. As we grow, we get to see right in front of our eyes that things do work together for our good, even if it isn't in the way we thought it would. The hard truth is that the good we want isn't always the good we need. Retrospect allows us to see that the way things worked out might not have been the way we planned, but it's still great. I don't know about you, but I don't want to finally allow myself to rest in these truths when I'm eighty. I really hate the phrase "You can sleep when you're dead." I don't want to start leading a trusting life decade down the road because I stubbornly feel like I need time to see that things will be okay. The things that make no sense to me now might when I'm eighty. That's comforting. I would rather my life prove my heart than my skin prove my age, wouldn't you?

# Chapter Ten
## Life Stages

### *Different Life Stages*

As a kid it's hard to understand how many ways you can go about living. For the most part, all throughout childhood, our peers are in indistinguishable life stages from our own, and there's a somewhat typical experience that most of us can relate to. The kids you grew up around and the things that connected us all were usually very similar. Of course we were our own people, but our lives didn't differ much from one to the next, especially where I'm from. The pace of life and certain transitional time markers were kept in step with those around us. We could look over to our classmate or peer and see that we're okay and "on track." Validation was somewhat easy to seek because there really wasn't that much competition, or if there was, it was over who got the best grade or who had the best car which were things I could care less about. It never felt like anyone was truly falling behind. There wasn't much room to feel like others were passing you by.

I've never felt like I was falling back until now. I'm just beginning to see how different life can look from one person to the next, which inevitably leaves the door wide open for comparison. The great thing about life that I have to constantly remind myself is that it isn't a race. Life is not a race. There is no winner. Why does it feel like that, though? Who cares if someone gets married sooner than you, gets promoted before you, or is able to buy a house years before you can. Just because someone gets what they've been working for and shares it sooner than you do, doesn't mean you're behind, slow, or doing something wrong.

We want our lives to prove our worth, and can't help but want physical things to show it. There isn't anything fundamentally wrong with that, but when that's the only way you feel validated, at one point or another, that method will seriously fail you. I hope you don't think because I say these things and believe them, doesn't mean I don't ever struggle with them. Of course I do, frequently. What I have learned is that insecurity is so exhausting and way too hard to keep up with. I do not want to lead a life of exhaustion just because I wish I had someone else's success, or looked like they do. That sounds like an absolute nightmare, but a lot of us do that.

After high school, especially, I was on a relentless pursuit to better myself and only participated in things that helped me get there. Since I did so much work to rid myself of insecurity and doubt to the best of my ability, I now hate when I feel this way. That might seem obvious—to hate doubting yourself—but I think some actually like it. It's easier and more comfortable to self-deprecate than it is to recognize how incredible you are. When someone gives a compliment, what's the first thing most people say. "No, but thank you," or "Oh, really?" We don't love recognizing how great we are, but what's so wrong about that?

Yes confidence can quickly slide into arrogance and pride, or worse, narcissism. Finding that balance is key, and I'm confident not because of my own ability but because of God's. What's hard about this life stage as opposed to the previous, is no longer can I look around to my peers or people around my age, because none of us are doing the same thing. Who is to say what the right path is? There is a lot of ways to live a good and fulfilling life but the only way to find out is to go and live yours. I don't know if it's a great realization or a sad one that life is a never-ending process, and you know what made me finally register this truth? Watermelons.

When I was little I grew them in the backyard, and loved to eat it. Sadly I am allergic now. Planting the seeds and going outside every day to water and check on them with my family was much more fun than getting to cut the fruit off of its stem and eat it. From what people seem to say, accomplishing the goal is never as great as it seems when you're trying to achieve it. Finishing is important, but that's not what makes it all worth it. Life is about showing up and creating the rhythm of going outside to check on the watermelon every day. Not about getting to eat the watermelon for five minutes. Most of life's memories are made in the process, not the satisfaction of it. It was not about enjoying the fruits of my labor; it was the labor that I remember. The best things in life aren't things, and if they were, it would actually make life a lot easier.

## *Resistance*

Have you ever felt almost a tangible tension in your mind between two things, where one thought pattern is clearly better, yet it's too hard to resist the other? If you deal with anxiety, you know exactly what I'm talking about. I know if I start to let myself go down the path of irrationality, it's going to be very difficult to pull myself out if it. There's a brief, almost instantaneous, moment where I decide which way I'm going to turn, and if I oblige my anxiety and go down that path, it's hard to turn around. Often times the unhealthy thinking pattern is easier because it's what we're used to. In my experience, the more you avoid what you're afraid of the worse your anxiety gets. What I do know now, though, that is the more you resist fear, the less it'll come knocking. It's too easy to fall into the never-ending pit of doubt than to rise above it into self-assurance. To desist less than helpful thought patterns, although difficult, will ultimately put you in a better place as opposed to succumbing to the lies that are too easy to believe.

To watch peers walk into their jobs, get married, or have x amount of money saved and feel like I'm nowhere near any of that is extremely hard, to put it mildly. I can't even pretend like it doesn't bother me because it does. I know that is only hurting me though. For my own good I need to stop fighting where I'm at, and trust that I've been placed exactly where I am for a reason. Resisting the lies that are at times so pervasive, and choosing to live in peace during a time that feels very chaotic is brave.

I'd say most doubt themselves in a specific area. Maybe their appearance, job, family, or financial status. My own doubts about myself have varied greatly as I've gotten older; they aren't as physical any more. Now as a college graduate most of my immediate doubts are careers based. The uncertainties regarding romantic relationships I try to put out of my head because it is not that pressing to me, but I would be lying if I said it doesn't come to mind frequently.

Adults have told me my entire life I'm mature for my age, so as you can imagine, teenage boys and then typical college frat guys and I never mixed well. Genuinely like oil and water. There's a narrative, for whatever reason, especially in the South, that you'll meet "the one" in college, and if you don't, good luck out there in the real world because as each day goes by the harder it'll get to find someone. Ring by spring, I'm sure you've heard of it. I can tell you from experience, a lot of girls now do not attain that status nor want it. Of course, people date seriously during this time and it can certainly end in a happily ever after. Other times it can crash and burn, I've seen both more than once. Why is quality so hard to find?

Let's just get this out of the way. I've never had a boyfriend, and I just turned twenty-two last week. (I'm now editing this a year later, still no boyfriend.) I'm sure some who are reading this will feel bad for me, embarrassed for me, wonder what's wrong with me, or can't believe I'd share that. That's fine to wonder. I have felt it all and have felt ashamed of the things I haven't done or experienced as well. That's the wildest thing about shame. It will linger behind every type of person and experience if you let it. It feels as if I'm not qualified or adult enough, like I can't have a real say in a situation that revolves around this topic because I don't have most of the experiences people my age have by this point.

I'm secure in who I am and don't need or want a relationship to make me feel complete. I don't want a status to make me feel worthy of something special. I know and believe that I am without that label. For that reason, I have no trouble telling you such. Oh, I almost forgot to mention this, I've never been kissed! Just thought I'd tell you so you feel extra sad for me:) This next sentence might sound really conceited and maybe borderline narcissistic, but give me a moment. One of the many reasons I hesitate this kind of relationship is because I know how amazing I am and don't want someone to change that. I love who I am as an individual and I'm concerned that once someone comes into my life, I'm going to change—that I'm going to lose a part of myself. I am sometimes too aware of the fact that the people you surround yourself with change you for better or worse. People, but especially in a romantic relationship, absolutely do not leave you neutral. I take it very seriously who I encircle myself with because it matters. They have a significant influence on who I am becoming.

On a more practical note, it also just seems so incredibly tiresome to have to think and worry about another person as much as I do myself. You don't have to tell me how this sounds, I'm well aware. I also see perfectly clear the fact that I'm seeing all of the potential negatives and maybe ignorantly ignoring the potential positives that could change me for the better. Loving someone in this manner feels like I'm simultaneously agreeing to loss, and loss is what I'm ultimately most afraid of. Why open myself up to something like this? Being linked to a person changes you forever.

I tend to be that way sometimes—actually most of the time. I think way too much and don't like letting myself feel. At the beginning of a relationship (again, I'm assuming because, remember, I've never been in one), you *feel* like you love the person but it hasn't been long enough to know that you do. After you've been in said relationship for a while and you know who they really are, when they're annoying or rude or not acting like themselves, you still love them because you know the way they're presenting isn't who they really are. At that point, you can still be frustrated and know you love them, despite whatever it is they're doing or however it is you're feeling.

The only thing that gets you to that point, though, is time. At first, you have to feel it and that doesn't sound extremely fun to me. I'm laughing at myself as I type this, this is just another example of how I sometimes feel like I see so much of the world backwards. Maybe it's because I'm left-handed, and in many ways, the world literally does feel that way. From listening to others, it seems like the beginning of a relationship is so much fun. They love the lust and the butterflies, and all the intense feelings that really only seem to be the most prevalent at that point. Not me, though. I want to be old and annoyed with a person I've been in a relationship for decades with. You can't think your way into loving someone, though. You love by doing, and that is a little hard for me to digest.

## <u>Look at People as Children</u>

People are annoying and they always will be. Yes, you're annoying. We all are. People disappoint us and do not meet expectations all of the time. What is ironic is how we give kids so much room to disappoint and annoy us and adults almost none. We automatically assume kids will mess up because they're learning, but adults are too! We expect adults to hold it together twenty-four hours a day, seven days a week. Obviously adults should not be were treated like children in most regards, but I'm more so talking about the permission to mess up, to try new things, and to go for the dreams that seem out of reach. For whatever reason, those things become less and less acceptable as you age.

Let's not forget about grace too. With guidelines, we allow kids to wonder, create, and, navigate, the world for themselves in whatever way is possible. We'd never want to squish a child's dream, but an adults? We do that all of the time without even realizing it. Why is the fuse for adults infinitely shorter than ones with kids? I heard this on a podcast years ago and haven't forgotten it since, to look at adults as children. Why? Because we are all still that person.

Whenever I'm frustrated with someone or need a fresh perspective, I try to imagine them as the innocent little kid they once were. This always leads me to a softer outlook than before, and it makes it a little easier to give them the benefit of the doubt. We're all human and make frequent mistakes, no matter how well you think you're holding it together.

### *This is the age*

Life is always full of questions, but this age feels even more so. I've questioned things my entire life, probably more so than the average person, but this feels different. I've started to dig deeper and ask myself if I believe and do the things I do because I actually believe in them, or did someone else influence the way I thought and I just followed suit. Clearly as children we need help with this because we cannot come up with belief systems on our own yet. Now I can though. These types of questions are not the kind I want to brush off because it doesn't apply but now it does. I guess I could but why would I want to push off the inevitable, and come to realizations that are possible now?
Questions like what do I want to be known for are weighted, complex, and can be answered so many different ways. No one can tell you the best, most efficient, and pain free way to go about your path and that is scary. In high school or even up to a certain point in college, when asked what you want to do responding with "I don't know" is perfectly acceptable. Before now, when I thought about that question, I could kind of avoid it because it did not need to be answered immediately. Now, when asked this same question, I feel people expect me to have a relatively solid answer. To be an adult means confronting big questions, make plans, and actively pursue them. Just last week, I was getting

coffee with a friend and she said, "At what point do you stop pretending to be an adult and you just are one?"

## *Smoke and Mirrors*

The world we live in now is the definition of smoke and mirrors, "The obscuring or embellishing of the truth. A situation with misleading or irrelevant information." Countless times I've asked myself, especially the past few years is, is the information I'm hearing the absolute truth or opinion based? What is the source? Is everything relative? If you want to spiral quickly ask yourself these questions. What's hard about this is, in most any given scenario, there are typically three truths. Your own truth, their truth, and the truth. All three can and tend to be different. One of my longtime friends says this, "I believe there is absolute truth but we cannot know it absolutely." I wish everyone would acknowledge that.

As a child, all of my questions were answered by my parents to whatever extent it needed to be with what they knew or what was appropriate at the time. As I got older I realized a large chunk of what people believe, even my parents, is based on an opinion. Most kids think everything their parents say is fact and nothing but. Then you grow up and realize it's not always that simple.

One of the biggest perception changes I had in college was how I viewed my parents—when I saw them for them as people. Growing up I never really saw them scared, sad, regretful, or unsure. They were just mom and dad and they always seemingly knew what they were doing. They were so steady, which I am incredibly grateful for. I never saw them as the flawed humans that they are. I couldn't imagine my parent's life before mine, like theirs only started once I came into it. Very egocentric I know. It's hard because kids clearly shouldn't know everything that goes on between their parents and the struggles they face, but with that, kids seldom if ever regard their parents' feelings because often times how they really are isn't shown to them at all. Or there is the other end of the spectrum where parents show their kids way too much and burden them with things they shouldn't. Most kids say whatever they want to get something from or out of them even if it's hurtful because they can seemingly handle it. Clearly, I do not know for sure, but having kids seems to be like signing up for the greatest love you'll ever know, but simultaneously agreeing to have your heart shatter into a million pieces at one point or another. At least, that's what my parents say.

Looking back and remembering the awareness I thought I had, the reality I thought was true as a child, and years later learning that wasn't how it really was is a trip. Certain relationships I saw right in front of my face were not as easy and great as they seemed to be. My parents were not the innocent and flawless young adults I thought they once were. Being at the age where my parents made decisions I wouldn't have is weird to think about. To now slowly begin to understand the reality of their own life, and how that was reflected onto me and my sister is something I never purposely thought about but naturally just happened. Would I have even liked the younger version of them? Would we have been friends? Seeing your parents as they really are, not this idyllic and sterilized version that most of us get as a child, is formidable in a way that's hard to express.

As kids we don't know that though. We can't see the whole picture. No matter how many detailed stories we get about our parents' lives before us, we will never fully be able to understand it. Some kids are lucky enough to live in a dreamy world where their parents seem pretty close to perfect, in a reality where you don't question them. I lived in that space, and only within the past few years have I thought about where I come from and how it is influencing the way I choose to live my life.

With infinite options on how to act, live, and believe, it can be hard to know who to really listen to and trust. That's one of the impossible choices we have in this life to trust and be willing to lay ourselves down, opening ourselves up to potential hurt but also deep connection and love, or shut everyone and everything out, and never experiencing the intimacy we all crave. Those are really the only choices we have. It feels scary to be someone with a perfectionistic and anxious nature, and to realize that facts and opinions can get very hazy, especially in the culture we live in now.

The most extreme version of this was displayed during the pandemic, which caused an exorbitant amount of anxiety that many were exposed to. People that never had an ounce of noticeable anxiety suddenly were infested with it. Fear is the greatest thief no one has seen but have all been stolen from. That kind of global fear was something no one had felt or experienced before. Where do you turn when nobody has an answer? It's funny because life has always been that way, no one knows all of the answers, but the pandemic really shoved it in everyone's face. Nothing could excuse anyone from the crisis that was happening. It was a guttural fear at times—that pit in your stomach that occurs when you can't believe what's going on around you. How could you not experience anxiety and depression with the constant and grim stimulation that was impossible to get away from.

We try to play God all the time, I know I do. One of the many reasons the pandemic shook everyone was the total stripping of control. The plans we thought were so stable before suddenly were anything but. Surrender was a huge lesson for everyone, one that we all desperately needed. I try so hard to find God in the answers and constantly ask Him to give me reasons for everything. I'm in the process of learning that He meets us in the questions, and that's just as powerful. If not more so than the answers.

## Chapter Eleven
### It's Never Too Late

If you have people in your life that tell you to go after your dreams and that you're capable enough to accomplish them, you're lucky. A support system is necessary because, when the hard days naturally come, they can help sustain the dream when it feels too heavy to carry. These people create a safety net beneath when you it feels like you're falling. Life happens, dreams defer, and the longer the clock keeps ticking, the harder it is to believe in yourself and the people around you. Suddenly it doesn't seem worth what could be on the other side. To feel like there is no other option but to reimagine the future you hoped for, because what you wanted or worked for never comes to fruition is a sad reality. It feels like losing something you never had.

As a culture we don't emphasize gradual success and improvement; we only enjoy seeing the finished product and celebrate that. We don't like or think to acknowledge incremental and steady growth because it's boring. We are much more fascinated with the rare story of instantaneous wealth and fortune. I think we forget that is the exception not the rule. Why do things seem to be the most ideal when they happen as fast as possible? A meaningful life is an unhurried one, but the world is characterized and celebrated by who can hurry the most. What if life feels so fast because we are the ones running at that pace? Would time slow down if we did? As we've all heard the best things in life take time. Young people especially hold themselves back because they're afraid if they don't have some sort of advancement quickly, they've failed, so then they settle. This is the age where we are so desperate to put our identity in something, anything, that when what we want doesn't work out (which is probably often) it is tempting to go for the lower hanging fruit.

Jim Carrey, in a speech he once gave, said something very profound that continually reminds me to keep striving even when I want to give up. He said, "You can fail at what you don't want, so you might as well take a chance on doing what you love." To be willing to risk failure for what you love is just as inspiring as the success itself. I aspire to be like the people that are open-handedly willing to accept failure in pursuit of their dreams, because most people are not willing to do that.

I've noticed recently the dichotomy in the pace of a Christian's life and a non-Christians life. Something I've noticed in the lives of others around me and watching it from afar on social media. You know the famous Christians that preach everything in God's timing, yet seem to be the ones rushing the most. Quick! Get married when you're twenty, get the house (a huge one at that), and have all the kids. Why, out of all of the people I know and listen to, the people that follow God fervently, outwardly seem to be the ones that are driving full speed ahead. Some might even say hurrying. The kind that preach to millions and say trust God fully and his perfect timing. That God is all you need, yet in a lot of ways, they are the ones that seemingly have it all. And have attained it quite early at that.

On the contrary, it seems there is another group of individuals who don't care at all about God or his timing, and have an almost spiritual ease and trust that if and when it happens, great. If it doesn't, they will still be okay. Having the security of a significant other, a house, a job, and kids is not bad. Attaining these things earlier than some absolutely does not mean you're rushing, but we know that waiting is the ultimate tester of faith. It is what builds deeper relationship with God, because our dependence on him becomes much more apparent. Time and time again the legends of the Bible, the people that changed history forever, were the people that waited to such a degree that we probably will never fully experience or understand. We are told that "Suffering produces perseverance, perseverance, character; and character, hope…" Suffering does that. Not status. It's too easy to say God is enough when you have more than you could ever need. These are the people God has previously used the most. Why today does it seem like the opposite? Like the people God has called to pastor generations are rich, famous, and beautiful. If we were all really honest with ourselves most of us just want God to bless our desires. And he loves to do that! But if that's why you follow God you are sorely missing out on the best part. Are you truly just after a relationship with God and becoming more like him, or that plus what he can give?

God doesn't work on our clock, and he exists outside of time, which is so infuriating at times. I don't want to water down what God is doing within me just because I'm comparing my life to everyone else's. As Thomas Merton says, "The biggest human temptation is to settle for too little." That feels tempting during such an uncertain time like the present.

On the other hand, you see fifty-year-old starting ventures and thinking they have all the time in the world to begin again, to start something new. Why are twenty something's so aware of their age and feel like time is running out of their hands like sand? That mentality needs to be continually cultivated amongst older adults, so younger ones can look to them and have the courage to step out beyond the realm of comfortability. The pressure to succeed and have an impressive list of accomplishments before the age of thirty feels so real to me. Why thirty? Who made that number out to be horrifying? I'm very worried that if I don't have my ducks in a row by that time I have wasted my twenties, and I'm a failure. I know this is dramatic and not reality, but if you want to come into the mind of a twenty something, that's what we're all thinking.

I wonder if we strive for such things to get the recognition we long for, rather than actually caring about the thing we're posting. I think that's a reason burnout is so rampant. So many get into what they're doing for the wrong reasons and cannot sustain the hard parts of whatever it is because they don't really care. Intention matters. I don't believe we do things just to do them—there's a reason for everything.

Once we slowly let go of other people's perceived judgments', (which probably are not there in the first place), we might realize that the only time limit we have is the one we're placing on ourselves. It's never too late for anything; I really do believe that even though the everyday wants me to believe the opposite. Don't let pride get in the way of what you know is right for you, and allow the supernatural to intercede in whatever capacity you are praying for.

At some point or another, we have all had dreams that felt too far-fetched. Maybe someone told you you'd never be able to make it into medical school or you would never be able to have kids, that there's no way you'd make it as an actor. When I experience rejection, which is a lot, I try to channel it into a place that launches me forward to continue trying, instead of backing down because of someones no. When my self-doubt gets to a level I'm not comfortable with, a question I ask myself is, "Is it really that unattainable?" When I start to question myself and think, "Why in the world did I choose to do something that constantly feels like an uphill battle," I remind myself that someone has to do it. So why can't it be me? If you've always wanted to learn how to play an instrument, do it. If you've always wanted to go back to school, go. Life is too short, and we shouldn't wait until it feels "right." There's no perfect time to do anything. I want to take advantage of every opportunity that comes my way because I can.

## The Journey Starts Within Yourself

The primary focus often seems to be what we can accomplish outwardly, but the conversation about what's progressing inwardly is sporadic and infrequent at best. We sometimes seem to care more about a big butt than we do about our big brain. Again and again we see people get to a point where they struggle to find fulfillment and worth, even when they seemingly have everything they could ever want. We've all been here, and if you haven't, you will. Not the having everything you want, but the struggle to find fulfillment in what you do, and worth within yourself. But for the rarities that do have it all, great body, great relationship, great job, they can't figure out why they're struggling, because outwardly, things look great. True growth and fulfillment starts within yourself, and very rarely is anything on the outside going to make you feel worthy and fulfilled on the inside.

What's frightening about that is what you don't transform, you transmit. If you choose not to do the work of finding deeper value outside of yourself, to focus your gaze on something higher, there is a good chance you will fall into a never-ending cycle of low self-esteem that might very well turn over onto other people. Self-loathing is contagious, and to get to a place of true confidence takes so much work. It comes from action. To change the thing that desperately needs changing means getting up and going. Having a blasé attitude toward working on whatever you need to work on is not realistic or feasible. No one gets better just because you think you want to. No one gets to a healthy, stable, and balanced place without copious amounts of effort. Digging and working through hard things isn't fun, and you can trust me when I say this, but the freedom that comes out on the other side is worth it. Discipline is never enjoyable in the moment but absolutely necessary for development.

### *Say Yes*

I say no a lot; my family and friends know this too well. I could list the excuses of why I think this is, but I'll spare you the time. We hear things like travel the path of least resistance, and that the safer and easier option is smarter. Without this overtly being said, I feel a lot of people think this way. If the path isn't clearly defined, it might not be right. That's not always the case, because, like I've said before, what even is safe? We all have a different barometer of safety which none of us are guaranteed anyway. Just because things make sense, seem safe, and check all the boxes doesn't mean you say yes. That's the narrative taught as you age: learn to make decisions that are realistic because you're in the real world now. That risky moves aren't for smart and wise adults. I was lucky enough as a child to not have had to immediately see how harsh the world can be. From as far back as

I can remember I've always felt like I could dream big. Which is rarer than I would have thought.

    I wrestled with the idea of moving back home after graduation, living with my parents and saving money, or moving to New York right after I graduated. One of the two options seemed much safer and I'm sure you can guess which one. Saying yes to something that's extremely unknown, even though deep down I know it's where I'm supposed to be, is scary. Scary doesn't even do it justice for how this feels. Never before have I been in a situation where I truly don't know what's next. Most of the change that I've gone through thus far has been calculated. Going away to college for four years was a change I had been preparing for essentially my entire life. I have never moved to a new city and not known when or if I would ever leave it. This is a change without a period at the end of the sentence. Some people like that; I'm coming to realize I don't. Or at least I don't right now.

    Until now, I haven't felt like I needed to put all of my trust in God because, honestly, my life has been so planned out and controllable. Correction it has felt planned and controllable, even though I know I've never had any real control over it. That's the problem when you have everything you need; you wrongly assume you have the power. Unfortunately we do not. There are times when we have to let go, and young adulthood is when that reality is thrown in your face.

    We think we control it all when good things are happening and subsequently take pride in it. If you believe such you're only looking at one side of the equation. What do you think when something doesn't go your way or tragedy strikes? Is it entirely your fault? We believe and accept we are not in control when bad things happen, but we seem to forget it when the good things are happening. That's what's nice about putting your trust in God; the pressure is off. Even though I know this it doesn't mean that I don't still feel and succumb to it at times. I hold the rope of control like it's a lifeline. What's so difficult about control is it's one of the hardest things to let go of, yet required to live the life God has for us.

# Chapter Twelve
## Tension of Opposites

Have you ever felt polar opposite ways about one thing? Antithetical emotions are very hard to articulate, and I particularly hate feeling two ways about something. It's difficult, especially in the middle of monumental moments, to know what to feel and how and when to express it. I never thought I would be sad or scared about growing up, but here I am. What's weird about that is I don't really know why I feel these things, because I know I am capable. I know I can do this and do it well. I don't fear responsibility. I have always liked having as much as I can get. Adult life has never felt foreign to me because for the longest time I've equated seriousness with adulthood. One of the reasons I was so excited to be grown was because of this assumption: that I didn't have to act like a fool because I'm not a child any more. I've always been full speed ahead and would dream of the time when I would no longer be stuck in the confines of childhood. Only now have I felt the desire to slow down.

### *Another Year*

You either love them or hate them; I fall somewhere in between the two. I love other people's birthdays but mine not so much. I have never liked when all of the attention is on me. My twenty-second birthday is next week, and I'm relatively excited about it. Birthdays without intention often result in reflection, reflection on the past year and what has or hasn't happened. Anxiety around my birthday hasn't been prevalent except for this one coming up. I'm very goal-oriented, so when another year rolls around and things I thought might've happened by now still haven't, I can't help but feel the slightest bit of embarrassment, sadness, or fear. What if another year goes by and I'm still in the same place? Staying stagnant is a huge fear of mine. Why, when you get older, do the years seem to go faster and faster? Twenty-two feels old, and I assume most people are laughing and rolling their eyes at that statement. I logically know I am very young, but the cliché that rings true for everyone: I never thought growing up would happen to me until it did.

The passage of time is impossible to grasp, and the more you think about it the harder it gets. Looking back at old pictures gives me the strangest feeling of *deja vu*. I remember some of those days so vividly I can smell it. It's crazy to look at that little girl and realize we're the same person. I just knew at that age I was destined to be a kid forever and that was it. So to the person who feels stuck, you aren't. It's one of the most universal things every person on the planet is under: time. With that though, the excitement in growing up has always been more prevalent in my life than the sadness of it dissipating. I have always seen the things that would be added to my life as I got older instead of the things that would consequentially leave. I've not felt true nostalgia about my childhood until now, and I don't know if I like this feeling.

Growing is not always fun and beautiful; sometimes it's heartbreaking and messy. Sadness has always made me uncomfortable, and I'm afraid if I let myself go there I'll end up in a pit that I can not crawl out of. Oh and crying, don't like that. As a child, I definitely correlated sadness and crying to weakness and sensitivity. If I'm honest I still do this, even though I know that is not true. In my mind if you're crying over someone or something they did, you're allowing them to control how you feel. I try so hard to not let other people dictate my emotions. Which in some ways might sound healthy, but the more I think about it the less I think that is true. People move us, that's just how it is. If I want to have deep and meaningful relationships with others I am also signing up for them to potentially hurt me very badly. The more you love someone the more they can hurt you.

    I like to think I'm tough, which in turn leads to me rarely showing my softer side. I love to joke that my heart is made of stone, but it's not. As a female this can be very challenging especially coming from the South. The stereotypical woman that is sought after is sweet, soft, and outwardly very loving to everyone they encounter. I am these things, but the first time you meet me I can almost guarantee you will not see that. To show those emotions, to me, is vulnerable. If you see that side of me I trust you a lot. This year has been different in so many ways. Feeling things I never thought I would, because I've always wanted to be where I am. I've never understood, until now, that things can be how you always wanted them to be, but it still doesn't feel like you thought it would. A lot of sentiment has accompanied this season of my life that has completely blindsided me.

## <u>Everything Matters and Nothing Does</u>

Some believe in coincidences, I do not. I trust that everything is God-ordained, so in that regard, everything matters. In the same breath, I know that this earthly life I live is temporary. Nothing can be taken into eternity. That makes trying to decide what matters today hard to decipher. It's funny to think about how hyper-focused we can get on the smallness of our own life. Most of the mundane things we care so deeply about do not matter at all. No one, shockingly, cares what you're wearing. And if we're honest with ourselves that's what consumes us most of the time, vain and unimportant things.

As a result, people are sometimes amused by my ability to detach. This might not be the best trait I possess, but in some ways I feel it's helped me. I understand that whatever most people worry about or mull over probably isn't life-altering. You might be confused because I've talked about my previous experiences with debilitating anxiety throughout this book, but my anxiety has always been very existential. The small worries most people struggle with I rarely deal with. The extreme anxiety I would see in a friend over finishing an assignment, thinking about an Instagram caption for an entire day, or what to wear to dinner is so insignificant to me that I genuinely cannot conjure up the energy to care. My anxiety has rarely, if ever, matched my peers. The things they worry about, I don't. The things I worry about, they don't. Well maybe not until now.

A funny anecdote, I am told as a baby I didn't care for pacifiers and as a kid, I was never attached to blankets or stuffed animals. I even asked my grandmother to make me a little blanket to hold at night so I could be like the other kids, but after a few weeks I was over it. I wish I lived in a reality where a piece of fabric made me feel safe. (Unlike my sister who carried around a foot-long stuffed worm her entire life and took it with her to college. His name was Wornie because when she was a baby she couldn't say Wormy. Although in Sunday school when I was a toddler I supposedly carried around a chair with me, can't really explain that!)

My friends laughed when I would cut off studying at night to go to bed even if I said I didn't feel prepared for a test the next day. In my mind, if I didn't prepare enough prior to my bedtime, it's no one's fault but my own. I'm not going to make my sleep suffer because of my lack of preparedness. Or when I was picking out decor for my apartment and would say "I don't care" apparently too often for my mom's liking, and she suddenly became extremely concerned with the fact that I didn't seem to care about it as much as she would hope. Don't get me wrong there are definitely times I need to care more, but generally people care way too much. That makes me look like I'm on the other end of the spectrum when I'm really not, or maybe I'm crazy and have attachment issues.

We've gotten it twisted in thinking that people care that much about us. No one cares about you as much as you do. Now yes, we all hopefully have people in our lives that love and care for us deeply, but I'm talking about all the others. The Instagram followers and the people in the grocery store, and the random people you cross on the street—I guarantee you they aren't thinking about your acne or the five extra pounds you've gained or your wrinkly clothes. Think about how much you worry about yourself and how conscious you have to be to consider others. Why would anyone else feel differently? We naturally think about ourselves first and foremost.

What has helped me significantly in navigating self-confidence is realizing that everyone is much more caught up in themselves than in me and my appearance. No one is thinking about me, in this regard, as much as I am. To think people are so concerned is arrogant. Don't think that what we do and say, how we treat others, doesn't matter because it absolutely does. Words, on the other hand, matter in a profound way. They have the ability to change the trajectory of someone's life, and that is huge. Be aware of the things that matter, like how you treat people, and let go of the things that are trivial, like whether or not you'll work out today. Don't be so utterly consumed in your own life that you can't zoom out and help the people that desperately need it.

## *Zoom Out*

The majority of the issues we face day to day come from being so zoomed in to our minor everyday problems. Tunnel vision can be very helpful in some scenarios but not always. Looking up and out beyond the everyday is vital to leading a peaceful life, or at least I think so. It's so easy to become inundated in our issues that we forget to acknowledge how much progress has been made. Life can be extremely overwhelming, that's no surprise to anyone. Zoom out, realize how far you've come, and be proud of yourself. This is something we don't do enough because it's wrongly seen as bragging, flaunting or whatever else you want to call self-recognition. Remembering how you persevered and how God got you through grants us the ability to put one step in front of the other when our feet get tired. I texted my mom the other day, and asked her how I got here just weeks before my college graduation. Her answer was short and sweet just like her. She said, "You kept going." That's how I got here.

## *Black and White*

By the cover of this book you can see how much I love black and white. Once I start to think about something, especially if it causes me stress, it's then very hard for me to move on and forget about it. I tend to want to live my life in an all-or-nothing type of way, but that isn't feasible for anyone nor is it the healthiest way to be. I tried that once. I don't consider myself to be a competitive person, but deep down, I think I might be. It's not often with people though; I more so compete with myself because I know I can always be better than I am. I don't settle, sometimes to a default, so this leaves me in a place where not much measures up to my standards. This is not serving me as much as I thought it would.

As months pass by where I apply to literally hundreds of jobs and receive offers from none, I feel as if I'm floundering aimlessly day after day. I feel like a complete looser and unless I'm actively doing something productive to change this narrative, I feel slight guilt for relaxing. I know I'm not the only one who feels like this. It's extremely disheartening when you think you know which way to go, but no matter what you do nothing seems to be heading in that direction.

It's claustrophobic, like I'm stuck, and don't know how I'm going to get out of this situation that I didn't choose in the first place. Am I delusional in thinking I'm capable enough to do what I want to do? I keep telling myself that knowing "the plan" isn't what makes me grounded as a person even though it feels that way. This doesn't mean I do nothing and wait for everything to come to me, absolutely not. I'll make the next right move with the knowledge and access I have now. That is all I can do, and it has to be good enough.

## *Social Media*

Social media will absolutely rule your life if you let it; notice I didn't say ruin. I think it's odd how we so easily will blame almost every bad habit or bad thing on it. These platforms are neutral; they do not have souls and they don't have feelings. They are not inherently bad. We make the choices we do. Not the phone. Ultimately, you are the one clicking the icon and scrolling for hours.

One challenge that we're all faced with when dealing with these platforms is whether you're fifteen or fifty; someone else, and probably not even someone you know, has the power to make you feel like you're inadequate. Like you could be doing so much more. Yes, people are behind the app, but that in and of itself is not what's causing you distress. It doesn't have the power to do that. Does social media have the potential to make it easier to allow bad habits and negative thought patterns into your life? Yes, but if a negative comment you see doesn't become the fleeting thought it should, that's slightly on you. You cannot blame social media entirely for that. Take some ownership in the things that bother you and understand you have the power to change the narrative you're telling yourself.

The current struggle I'm facing with when dealing with social media is the pace of everyone else's life compared to mine. Not what it is they're actually doing, but the speed at which things seem to be happening for them. I realize I have nothing but time to figure out what I want to do and who I want to be, but it doesn't feel like it. Why is that? It seems like everyone else my age is ahead of me. Often times to launch forward we first have to stop. Have all generations struggled with the pace of which others' lives seem to be happening? It's hard to fully comprehend how social media has allowed us to see virtually anyone and everyone's lives—that is crazy if you really think about it. To be able to see what everyone deems important and how they are accomplishing that is cool and inspiring to some degree, but too easily leads to questions about our own desires that would not have been there before.

I know my worth isn't found in what I do, but why can't I have both? Why can't I know my value doesn't come from a successful career but also have a successful career? That's where a lot of us fall; we want both. We say we'll believe we have value when we get the job, the relationship, the house. That's not how it works though. The way you think about yourself won't change unless you realize your value now. You will never find purpose in what you're doing unless you realize it now.

I don't want to just believe God is good when there are very obvious physical blessings that prove it. That's infantile faith: not seeing the value in refinement and the good in the waiting. It's like when you are little and think you only have a good parent when they allow ice cream after you get a shot. (This is what immediately came to mind because there was a frozen yogurt shop right underneath my pedestrian's office.) The shot hurts but is necessary. That momentary pain, permitted by your parent, allows you to live a healthier, safer, and longer life later. The life you can't yet see but is being cared for in the present by something uncomfortable.

## *Plans*

I love to plan just as much as the next person. I come from a family that thrives off of them, and as I've gotten older, I make "the plan" most of the time. We all have those people in our lives that lead the pack, and when it's time to decide what to do, you look at them. When someone doesn't know what to wear, what to do, or wants advice, I tend to be the one people come to because I shoot straight. I'm decisive, know what I want, and am typically confident while doing it. All of that said, though, pride is my downfall and sometimes I'm overly confident. Working on that...

This sounds great to think you know what you want, but it's created some unhealthy all-or-nothing thinking when I think about future plans. I have this idea that I'll go to New York, live there for a while, have a wildly successful career, and eventually settle back in Nashville. That could happen and I pray it does. We all know that the way we think things will go is seldom how it goes. As someone with big aspirations, the thought of failing is that much more. I've put so much unnecessary pressure on myself to do big things, and the thought of it not working out is terrifying. Ideas like I thought I knew the direction God was leading me in, how could I have messed that up? What did I do wrong? These kinds of things keep me up at night.

I might be missing the point though. To think that I'm failing because I don't have immediate success is nonsense. Who cares if I go to New York for a year and end up coming back to Nashville. That doesn't mean that New York and my plan failed me. This city is a magical place and to have the opportunity to live here, even if it's for a short time, is worth it. To get here, stay here, and then maybe even make it here is something most people are too afraid to try. This is a place where the wildest of dreams come true, and if they don't you try and try again. You pivot and keep going because the city never stops. It doesn't wait for you. This is one reason I love it so much: people are always getting up and starting over. It's a place where I feel brave, capable, and strong. Adjectives that, for the longest time, I would not use to describe myself. For me to thrive in a place where a lot of people think they can't make me feel able.

With the boundless unknown in front of me, I realize I need to give myself space to breathe and to be okay with contradicting myself because I'm not a robot. It's hard for me to make a plan or think I know what I believe in or want, and then change my mind. This comes from the all or nothing thinking. I do not like changing my mind. I feel like a fraud when I do that even though I know that's untrue. Making mistakes and changing your mind frequently is normal and part of life especially during young adulthood. No one is keeping a record of what I've said and done; that's all on my own doing. We allow shame and fear to dictate our next steps, but God doesn't put that on us. Enjoy the day that's been given to you today. *S*top thinking about what your days used to look like, or what you believe they should look like. Choosing to be in the past or future mindset is too easy. We're called to more.

# Chapter Thirteen
# When Nothing Seems to Work Out

### *If I'm honest*

I'm not the most empathetic person you'll ever meet, and if I don't reign it in, I see the world through an extremely critical lens. Because of this I used to question, okay judge, the people that moved back in with their parents and struggled to get a job directly after graduating. I so wrongly assumed that the reason it took them longer to get on their feet was due to their work ethic, or that their drive wasn't as high as the people that did obtain some sort of position immediately. If I'm brutally honest with myself, I might have even called them lazy and definitely never thought I would end up in that position.

Part of the problem is wrongly thinking it's all about me,. That getting a job is one hundred percent in my own hands, and if I can't acquire one easily or quickly it's all my fault. I know the plans of God are never stagnant, and He is constantly working in ways I can't possibly know about yet or understand. I've stepped into many people's realties, one I didn't volunteer for, and am being changed in ways that would've been impossible if not. I feel myself becoming more empathetic day by day, which believe me, is something I needed to learn. When you're taking all of the right steps and doing everything you can and things still don't work out, then what?

I have quoted Dietrich Bonhoeffer earlier in this book, but this is too good not to share, because this is how my life feels right now. He proclaims, "God's cause is not always the successful one, that we could really be 'unsuccessful' and yet still be on the right road. But this is where we find out whether we have begun in faith or in an act of enthusiasm." The only answer that makes sense to me is that there are real limitations on us that only the supernatural can intercede for. That all things are working together for the good of that the person in due time, but that's much easier to believe when things are going your way.

## *Back to Square One*

All of my plans crumbled. I was going to sign on an apartment with a roommate and move to New York in August of 2022. I was applying to jobs left and right, and one that I thought might work out decided to go on an indefinite hiring freeze. The roommate I thought I had decided on backed out twenty-four hours before we planned to leave. I quickly regrouped and made plans to move in with a different roommate months later which, you guessed it, fell through too.

What am I supposed to do? I've made peace with a plan I deeply feel is from God, yet every which way I go the door shuts or doesn't even open at all. I have had no choice but to pivot and reconsider what I really want. Fear naturally has been involved in this process, and a small amount is healthy because it motivates us to keep going. But if you don't have a steady hand on the fear barometer it will lead to unbelief and doubt. Fear leads to doubt, and once you doubt long enough, it'll turn to deep disappointment and maybe even despair. I know I don't want that.

Why is this so hard? God, why are you not opening the doors I thought you wanted open? Then I remembered this book. And yes I pray it lends you some sort of insight, but to be honest it is mostly for me. I wanted to write about the growing pains of young adulthood but truthfully did not want to experience it for myself. The most valuable lessons learned are the ones we personally experience at a guttural level. I wanted, just like everyone else, an easy transition into adulthood and have a dream scenario the second I graduated. To have a vision that forces you to take the long and scenic route will be worth it, I'm sure of it, but that makes today really hard.

When these said plans fell I had a quick but impactful lapse of judgment that has turned into one of the best stories of my life yet. My first few moments in a "professional job" (completely unrelated to digital media because I thought I should seek out something stable) did not go well. When the move to New York date got pushed back I suddenly went into turbo mode and thought I needed to get any sort of job as soon as possible. I took marketing classes along with my creative ones in college, so for the time being, I decided I would try to get a marketing or sales job because those are stereotypically easier to get than an art or creative-based one.

Quickly after applying to these random and off the wall jobs that I did not care about, I got an interview for a role that was presented one way and completely different from what it actually was. Do your research on companies before you agree to work for them, rookie mistake. During the interview process I was told I would be going to events around Nashville as a representative for various non-profits to acquire potential donors. It wasn't a desk job and the pay was better than nothing, so I said I would give it a go knowing it would be very temporary. At that point I was desperate to get out of my own head and do something. Days later I was offered the position and on my first official day I mustered up the willpower to go. I had on a cute outfit and was willing to give it my best.

I arrive and the first thing I am asked to do is put on a T-shirt with farm animals on it. I quickly change, slightly concerned at this point, and go into the training room. Now typically for a job there is a lengthy training period. Second red flag, the first being the farm animal shirt, was the fact that my "training period" was twenty minutes long before I went off to my work sight for the day. I am assigned a location, along with a few other people, and they tell me I am going to Walmart. There is nothing wrong with Walmart, but this particular one is not in a good part of town. That plus when they told me I would be going to "events," I did not foresee Walmart as the location. I continue on determined not to quit within the first hour, because truthfully I just wanted to see what would ensue for the rest of the day. You know when you're in a situation and realize what is about to happen will make for a great story later? This was one of those moments.

I arrive at Walmart and am told we will be setting up a tent in the parking lot. Not only am I working this "event" at Walmart, it's taking place in the parking lot. Mind you it is the middle of July in Tennessee so it is very hot and humid. I quickly realize I have been bamboozled into this job and need to abort. Alas, I stick it out the rest of the day only for the fun of it, where a homeless man sat under my tent just to have a rest, a policeman chased someone down in the parking lot, and to top it off at the end of the day, a man came up to me with a very serious look on his face and said, "Do you know who you're working for?" That's always a great sign. I informed my boss that I would be quitting after my one hard day of work in the Walmart parking lot with my cow T-shirt on. This lit a fire under me to never again settle and has given me quite the story to tell that always ensures tons of laughter.

## <u>When the Plan Turns to Shambles</u>

It's a weird place to be when all you know what you're doing involves today and tomorrow, and unless you've personally experienced this it's hard to explain how difficult it is. It's taking its tole on me and I'm tired. Not the tired like I need to go take a nap but the weary tired. I'm doing everything I know to and the pendulum has not swung at all. I'm scared. I'm so used to knowing my day-to-day and even what the next year of my life will look like. The trajectory of my post-college life hasn't been what I thought it would be when I was preparing for it. It's not bad but very different than what I would consider ideal. Isn't that how most of life goes? The cheesy saying that rings true for all of us is, "If you want God to laugh tell him your plans."

This is the first time in my life where growth has simultaneously felt like loss, maybe that's why it feels so hard now. Loss is something I've always been afraid of, yet also one of the first things I thought I needed to avoid. This might sound strange to some, but my food allergy was the first run-in I had with it, loss, even though for the longest time I wouldn't be able to vocalize it. It was the first time I understood that I would never have certain experiences that other people don't think twice about.

I can't just go into a bakery and pick out anything I want. I can't eat things where I don't know what's in it, and it's extremely difficult for me to be adventurous with new food. Whenever I go out to eat, I am trusting a stranger who I can't even see, to put food in front of me that won't cause me potentially great harm. Going to a restaurant is an act of faith. I will never be as care free about eating as some people get to be. My parents found out I was allergic to nuts when I was one year old so this is all I've ever known. There is loss there and it's sad. I was never told that until I was seventeen. My food allergy is actually a big reason why I ended up in therapy in the first place. One of the first things I did before desensitizing myself to my triggers was make peace with and grieve the fact that I have to deal with this for the rest of my life. We all have crosses to bear and this is one of mine.

No one has to remind me that food allergies are very common, especially today, and that yes it "could be worse." My day to day life is rarely affected by this, but the "It could be worse" phrase held me up for a long time. I completely disregarded my feelings about it being sad and at times extremely scary because I just kept telling myself someone somewhere has it worse than me. Is a food allergy a death sentence? Probably not. Does it suck? Absolutely. I would not wish food allergies upon anyone. In most situations it could be worse, that's the reality of most of them. What that does is disregard essentially everyone else's experience and makes them rethink how they feel. It can lead to distrust within yourself and make you wonder why you feel a certain way. It is completely bizarre that our culture measures and compares suffering. It is not a competition and it is something every living person has to deal with.

I think previous generations learned this, things could be worse, and typically what you learn is often what you preach because you don't know a better way. Until someone questions it. People didn't talk about their feelings and were "practical." It was the 'pull up your bootstraps and go' type of mentality. Now on the other side of the generational spectrum we might be creating and raising kids to be extremely soft. Just today in Nashville, school was canceled because of a high wind advisory. Now if it's windy we don't go to work?

Since when do we live in a world where we believed every single opinion must be shared? It does not take a genius to recognize that as humans we watch what people do before we listen to what they say. How do kids learn? They watch. That is how you teach and ultimately change people. Judgmental scolding does absolutely nothing, but that is all anyone seems to want to do. The previous generation didn't speak up enough and now my generation won't shut up. Can we win? What's the balance between recognizing loss, tolerating an appropriate amount of anxiety, and all the while not becoming inundated in any of it? Only when I recognized loss and faced my anxiety head on could I grow from and move past that place.

With the unforeseeable future and the endless possibilities that lie ahead of me, I feel loss in a way similar to my allergy. There are only a few times in life when you can appropriately use extreme words like never and always. This is one of those times. The way my life has looked these past four years will never be that way again. Ever. That's a lot of loss, but the possibility for what's to come makes it seem worth it—to peacefully close this sweet chapter and move on.

I can't wait to get to the place where my current struggles make even the slightest bit of sense. It seems like only once we've arrived do, we then talk about how we're thankful for the uphill incline, how it strengthened us. All of those questions are neither here nor there because now we see for ourselves that hindsight truly is 20/20. I'm trying to live in and celebrate the uphill battle that life takes me on, because majority of life is climbing. I need to learn how to enjoy it and not wish it away. To keep putting in work when it seems like nothing is changing is ridiculously hard, but I know there is power in consistency. I'm hopeful because we never know how the ball is rolling and how things are changing for the better that I can't possibly see until I get to the other side. Today might be the day that everything changes.

I cannot believe I'm about to make a dance analogy but here I go. As you know dance is constant movement. There are usually a few moments in a routine where you can somewhat catch your breath but they are far and few between. Especially if you are competing, which is where most of my experience lies, you pull out your best tricks and try to incorporate the most impressive skills to rack up the most points possible.

I'm sure you get the message that this time in my life feels like it's paused and without my consent—almost like it is a divine delay of sorts. It's like in the movies where someone's feet are stuck to the ground and the entire world is speeding around them, but they can't seem to figure out where to go and how to get unstuck. That's how I feel. When I think about my reality, all I want it to do is change. Every day I try to come up with something different to try and hurry my way out of the state my life is in. Not that it's so horrible, because it isn't, but it is so unknown. The longer it stays like this, the more restless and unsettled I become. One night this week, right as I was drifting into sleep, I had different thought about the state of my life, and weirdly dance came to mind.

As someone who's been in tons of dances myself and seen ten times that, I can tell you spectators very rarely remember what they saw or what you did in the dance. That being said, during the few pieces that have very intentional pauses, or a story, are the ones people remember. No one can ever recall what tricks you did, what you won, or the recognition you received. The pause, the moment when you seemingly aren't doing anything, the moment that feels like a throw away is sometimes the most powerful part. It catches people's attention because so few people do it. It means something and it's important, just maybe not in the way you would expect or hope for.

As I laid in bed thinking about this it seems comical how similar life is to that. "Life's a dance…" I never really understood that phrase until now. I so badly want my life to look a certain way. For it to be packed full of impressive things, people, and jobs. Then I quickly remember that ultimately my life isn't for me. My life is for Gods glory and he is going to use me in specific ways to bring other people to him. I'm laughing as I type this because it's so on brand for me, wanting to control my testimony. I want God to use me in the specific way that I come up with, but we don't get to choose that.

My reliance and faith in him to complete a good work in me isn't dependent on if I love or understand what he's doing. I want my life to show the fancy tricks and the most impressive skills, but I guess that isn't what I need or what other people need to see in me right now. This pause that feels so unnecessary, meaningless, and sometimes very embarrassing is not for nothing. Is it how I wish God was using me? Not really. But this is my story and the tiniest piece of his ultimate one. How I carry myself through, fully reliant on God, is what people will remember. Not the job I one day have or the people that surround me. These moments, the ones I'm living now, are the ones that I will talk about decades down the road as some of the most life changing experiences I will ever encounter; and I know that isn't meaningless.

I've started to contemplate one of the hardest questions and it's forced me to get really honest with myself. Is God still enough for me, will he fully and truly satisfy me, if I get nothing that I want. If I get nothing that I feel I deserve. Of course the quick and simple church answer is, "Of course!" But honestly sometimes it feels like no. It's funny to me how we strive for such overt blessings, which isn't right or wrong, they are good gifts from God and worthy of celebration. They are obvious factors that contribute to a good and meaningful life, but it isn't what makes you.

Struggle makes a person and God keeps a person. What if the hard moments, the awkward and painful in-between, was actually the blessing? Not many people get the opportunity to take a hard look at what they think about themselves, the world, and God, with little to no distraction, yet that is the position I am in. I would even argue the majority of people get to hide behind a career or a person and only decades later realize they're only satisfied, only okay, because of what they have or what they do—not because of who they are and who God is. Thanks to these moments and whatever God is up to now, that will not be me.

# Prologue
## I'm Ready

*"A journey of a thousand miles begins with a single step."*

I first began scribbling some words about growing up during the fall of 2021 and had no intention of my deepest thoughts becoming public, and now it's May of 2023 and I have been offered a publishing contract to a book that, in a lot of ways, feels like it wrote itself. A lot has happened since I graduated on that beautiful day in May of 2022, some of which I've shared in depth and some not as much. Countless job rejections, lots of traveling, births, deaths, weddings, holidays, family health scares, and a horrific school shooting that has changed my hometown forever. This past year has shaped me in ways that wouldn't have happened any other way if I was not at home, but now it's time to go.

I'm on a plane right now to LaGuardia without a return flight back to Nashville. I'm nervous because, yes, I know where I'm landing, but after that I'm not entirely sure what I'm doing, where I'm going, and how all of this will play out in reality. The thing about following your wildest dreams that no one talks about is that it's really scary and not always fun. It's the strangest feeling in the world when you know what you are doing is the best thing for you in the long run, but in the moment it feels so uncomfortable, so wrong. I love the idea of living an adventurous life and now I'm going to try and go live it the best way I know how. I'm not expecting this to be sunshine and rainbows all of the time, but I'm confident I will look back on this time with deep admiration, for maybe one day understanding just how big of a leap of faith I took.

All throughout my writing process I thought about how I was going to end the book, but every time I tried to think about how and when I got stuck. The truth is I don't know how to wrap this book up because my story is just getting started. I don't know the ending and that is okay—that's good. As you've just read, the only insight I have is through my own experience. I'm currently wrapping, cutting, and tapping pieces of my life together and trying to turn it into something meaningful. But that's ultimately God's job, not mine, and I have high expectations for Him to deliver in whatever capacity is best for me.

I also can't be certain that all of the anxiety, heartache, doubt, and self-reflection will be worth it in the end because I don't know that either. It's so surreal to realize that all of the adults you thought had it figured out way back then never really did. So I will see the beauty in the challenge, the hidden blessings in the desert, and refuse to believe that God is anything less than miraculous and showing up in major ways in my life. Because although this feels scary and unknown I know that because I'm walking with Him, I will not fail. I'm still growing, are you?

# Acknowledgements

*To Olympia and my editors*: I will never forget the morning I opened my email, in May of 2023, and saw that you would like to represent and publish my work. Thank you for believing in me, my vision for this book, and for giving me the platform to share it in partnership with you.

*Mom and Dad*: Thank you for allowing me to stand on your shoulders so I can reach higher than I ever thought possible. I would be nothing without you two and your endless love and support.

*Claire*: Although you're technically my younger sister, I look up to you in so many ways. My love for you is deeper than anything I could ever write.

*God*: I cannot end this book without acknowledging you. You are the ultimate author. Because your love is greater than life, I will praise you.